Dolomites for Every Season

Exploring the Best of the Dolomites, One Season at a Time

ERIC REED

TABLE OF CONTENT

WELCOME TO THE DOLOMITES

The Dolomites, a spectacular mountain range in northeastern Italy, are a treasure trove of natural beauty, adventure, and cultural charm. Known for their dramatic peaks, emerald valleys, and unique pink-hued sunsets, this UNESCO World Heritage Site attracts visitors from around the world. Whether you're a seasoned outdoor enthusiast or simply seeking a serene escape, the Dolomites offer something for everyone.

With their rich history, diverse ecosystems, and a blend of Italian and Ladin cultures, the Dolomites promise a travel experience like no other. The region is dotted with charming villages, world-class ski resorts, and scenic trails that wind through breathtaking landscapes. From the jagged spires of Tre Cime di Lavaredo to the gentle meadows of Alpe di Siusi, the Dolomites are a true masterpiece of nature.

In this guide, you'll find everything you need to plan
the perfect trip—whether you're visiting for a weekend, a
week, or longer. Get ready to explore the best destinations,
activities, and flavors the Dolomites have to offer. From
hiking and skiing to savoring local dishes and discovering
hidden gems, this book will be your go-to resource for making
the most of your time in these unforgettable mountains.

Why Visit the Dolomites?

The Dolomites are a destination that truly has it all:
breathtaking landscapes, endless outdoor activities, rich
culture, and a welcoming atmosphere. Whether you're a thrill-
seeker, a nature lover, or someone looking to immerse
yourself in history and tradition, here's why the Dolomites
should be on your travel list:

1. Spectacular Scenery

The Dolomites are renowned for their stunning landscapes,
featuring dramatic peaks, lush green valleys, alpine meadows,
and sparkling lakes. The region's unique geology creates a
mesmerizing palette of colors, especially during sunrise and
sunset, when the mountains glow in hues of pink and orange.

2. Year-Round Activities

No matter when you visit, there's something to do. In winter,
the Dolomites are a world-class skiing and snowboarding
destination with pristine slopes and cozy mountain refuges.
Spring and summer bring vibrant wildflowers, endless hiking
and cycling trails, and opportunities for climbing or
paragliding. Autumn offers tranquil scenery and golden
foliage, perfect for photography or quiet exploration.

3. Outdoor Adventures for All Levels

From family-friendly trails to challenging via ferrata routes, the Dolomites cater to every type of traveler. Explore iconic spots like Tre Cime di Lavaredo, Lago di Braies, or Seceda, or venture off the beaten path to discover hidden gems. The range of activities ensures that both beginners and seasoned adventurers will find something exciting.

4. Unique Blend of Cultures

The Dolomites are part of Italy but have a unique blend of Italian, Austrian, and Ladin influences. This multicultural heritage is reflected in the local cuisine, language, and traditions, creating a fascinating cultural experience alongside the natural wonders.

5. Culinary Delights

Food lovers will be in heaven with the Dolomites' delicious offerings. From hearty alpine dishes like polenta and canederli (bread dumplings) to fine wines and locally crafted cheese, the region is a feast for the senses. Don't miss the chance to enjoy a meal at a rifugio, where you can savor traditional flavors with a side of jaw-dropping views.

6. Easy Accessibility

Despite their remote beauty, the Dolomites are surprisingly easy to reach. Major airports like Venice, Verona, and Innsbruck provide convenient entry points, and excellent roads connect travelers to the region's main hubs.

7. Unparalleled Tranquility

While some areas are popular with tourists, the Dolomites still offer plenty of peaceful retreats where you can disconnect from the hustle of daily life. Explore quiet villages, serene alpine lakes, or secluded trails to reconnect with nature.

8. A UNESCO World Heritage Site

The Dolomites earned their UNESCO status for their extraordinary natural beauty and geological significance. Visiting this protected area allows you to experience one of the world's most remarkable landscapes while supporting its preservation.

Whether you're planning a short trip or a longer stay, the Dolomites promise an unforgettable experience that blends adventure, relaxation, and cultural discovery. This is a place that stays with you long after you leave.

Geography, History, and Culture of the Dolomites

The Dolomites are a striking mountain range located in northeastern Italy, spanning the regions of South Tyrol, Trentino, and Veneto. These peaks, part of the Southern Limestone Alps, are known for their rugged beauty and unique rock formations. This section explores the geography, history, and culture that make the Dolomites such a remarkable destination.

Geography

Location: The Dolomites cover an area of approximately 15,942 square kilometers and include some of Italy's most iconic natural landmarks.
Notable Peaks: The range features dramatic mountains such as Marmolada (the highest peak at 3,343 meters), Tre Cime di Lavaredo, and Rosengarten.

Geological Significance: Composed primarily of dolomite rock, the mountains are famous for their jagged spires, sheer cliffs, and distinctive pink glow at sunrise and sunset, a phenomenon known as *enrosadira*.
Biodiversity: The region boasts a rich variety of flora and fauna, with alpine meadows, dense forests, and wildlife like ibex, marmots, and golden eagles.

History

Early Settlements: Archaeological evidence suggests that humans have inhabited the Dolomites for thousands of years. The Ladin people, who still reside in the region, are descendants of ancient Rhaeto-Romanic tribes.
Medieval Times: During the Middle Ages, the area was influenced by various rulers, including the Roman Empire and later the Holy Roman Empire. Small mountain villages flourished during this period.
World War I: The Dolomites were a significant battleground between Italy and Austria-Hungary. Visitors can still explore tunnels, trenches, and museums that preserve this history.
UNESCO Recognition: In 2009, the Dolomites were designated a UNESCO World Heritage Site for their exceptional natural beauty and geological importance.

Culture

Languages: The region is linguistically diverse, with Italian, German, and Ladin being the main languages spoken. Ladin, a Romance language, is particularly unique to the valleys of the Dolomites.
Traditions: The Dolomites are rich in cultural traditions, from folk music and dance to centuries-old festivals like the "Krampuslauf," a winter parade featuring mythical creatures.

Architecture: Traditional wooden chalets and beautifully frescoed churches are hallmarks of Dolomite villages.
Cuisine: The local food reflects the region's cultural blend, with influences from Italian and Austrian gastronomy. Staples include speck (cured ham), knödel (dumplings), and hearty mountain stews.

The Dolomites' captivating mix of natural beauty, historical depth, and cultural richness makes it a place that feels both timeless and deeply alive. As you explore the region, you'll find that its geography, history, and culture are intertwined, offering insights into a way of life that has flourished for centuries in harmony with the mountains.

When to Visit: A Seasonal Breakdown

The Dolomites are a year-round destination, offering unique experiences with each changing season. Here's a guide to what you can expect during spring, summer, autumn, and winter, helping you choose the perfect time for your visit.

Spring (March to May)

What to Expect: Spring is a time of renewal as snow melts and the valleys come alive with blooming wildflowers. While higher altitudes may still have snow, lower trails become accessible.
Highlights:
Wildflower-covered meadows in Alpe di Siusi and Val Gardena.
Quieter trails and fewer crowds compared to peak seasons.
Crisp, cool air and photogenic landscapes.
Activities: Lower-altitude hikes, photography, and cultural festivals like Easter celebrations in local villages.

Considerations: Weather can be unpredictable, with a mix of rain, snow, and sunshine. Some mountain passes and facilities may still be closed.

Summer (June to August)

What to Expect: Summer is the most popular season, with warm temperatures, clear skies, and endless outdoor opportunities. The Dolomites' peaks and trails buzz with activity.

Highlights:
World-famous hikes like Tre Cime di Lavaredo and Seceda.
Via ferrata routes and mountain climbing for adrenaline seekers.
Vibrant cultural festivals, such as the Ladin St. Anne Festival in July.

Activities: Hiking, mountain biking, climbing, and scenic drives.

Considerations: Accommodations and trails can get busy, so book early. Afternoon thunderstorms are common—plan outdoor activities for the morning.

Autumn (September to November)

What to Expect: Autumn is a quieter, more tranquil time, with fewer tourists and stunning fall foliage painting the landscapes.

Highlights:
Golden larches and breathtaking autumnal scenery, especially in Val di Funes and Lago di Braies.
Cooler weather ideal for hiking and exploring.
Wine harvest season and local food festivals celebrating chestnuts, speck, and apples.

Activities: Hiking, photography, and exploring small, peaceful villages.

Considerations: Some lifts and facilities begin to close in late October, and temperatures can drop significantly, especially at night.

Winter (December to February)

What to Expect: Winter transforms the Dolomites into a snow-covered wonderland, making it a paradise for winter sports enthusiasts.
Highlights:
Skiing in world-class resorts like Cortina d'Ampezzo and Val Gardena.
Christmas markets in towns such as Bolzano and Bressanone.
Snowshoeing and sledding for family-friendly fun.
Activities: Skiing, snowboarding, snowshoeing, and festive village explorations.
Considerations: Popular ski areas can be crowded, especially during Christmas and New Year. Book accommodations well in advance for this peak season.

Best Time to Visit

For Outdoor Adventures: Summer and early autumn.
For Peace and Scenery: Spring and late autumn.
For Winter Sports: December through February.

No matter when you visit, the Dolomites offer something extraordinary to enjoy in every season!

PLANNING YOUR TRIP

Getting to the Dolomites (By Plane, Train, and Car)

Reaching the Dolomites is straightforward, with various transportation options depending on your starting point and preferences. Here's a guide to getting there by plane, train, and car.

1. By Plane

The closest airports to the Dolomites are:

Venice Marco Polo Airport (VCE): Approximately 2.5–3 hours' drive to the Dolomites.

Verona Villafranca Airport (VRN): About 3 hours away by car.
Innsbruck Airport (INN), Austria: A convenient option for those coming from the north, around 2 hours' drive.
Bolzano Airport (BZO): The nearest regional airport, but with limited flights.

Tips:

For international travelers, Venice or Munich Airport (4–5 hours' drive) often offers the best connections.
Car rentals are available at all major airports for flexibility.
Shuttle services are also available to key towns like Cortina d'Ampezzo, Bolzano, and Selva di Val Gardena.

2. By Train

Italy's efficient train network connects major cities to stations near the Dolomites. Key routes include:

Venice to Bolzano/Bozen: Travel via Verona for a scenic journey (3–4 hours).
Innsbruck to Bolzano/Brunico: A direct route from Austria, taking about 2 hours.
Milan to Trento/Bolzano: Approximately 3–4 hours by train.

From the train stations, buses or taxis provide access to mountain villages and resorts. Look for regional buses like Südtirol Mobil or Dolomiti Bus for connections.

Tips:

Book tickets in advance for better prices on long-distance routes.
Regional trains don't require reservations and run frequently.

3. By Car

Driving to the Dolomites offers the most flexibility, especially for exploring remote areas and scenic routes. Major access points include:

From Venice: Take the A27 highway north toward Belluno, then follow signs for Cortina d'Ampezzo or other destinations.
From Verona: Use the A22 Brenner Motorway (Autostrada del Brennero) and exit at Bolzano, Chiusa, or Bressanone for connections to Val Gardena or Alta Badia.
From Innsbruck: Drive south via the Brenner Pass on the A22.

Tips:

Some mountain passes, such as Passo Sella or Passo Gardena, may close in winter due to snow. Check road conditions in advance.
Parking can be limited in popular areas, especially during peak seasons. Look for public lots or accommodations with parking options.

Additional Transportation Notes

Shuttles and Transfers: Many private companies offer transfers from airports and train stations to the Dolomites. Options like Cortina Express or Südtirol Transfer are reliable.
Eco-Friendly Travel: The Dolomites promote sustainable tourism. Use buses, trains, and bike-sharing services where possible to reduce environmental impact.

Whether you arrive by plane, train, or car, the Dolomites are well-connected and accessible, setting the stage for an unforgettable trip

Transportation Options Within the Dolomites

Getting around the Dolomites can be as much a part of the experience as the destinations themselves. Whether you prefer driving, public transport, or eco-friendly alternatives, here's an overview of the best ways to navigate the region.

1. By Car

Driving is the most flexible way to explore the Dolomites, allowing you to access remote villages, scenic mountain passes, and trailheads.

Advantages:
Access to less-frequented areas and hidden gems.
Flexibility to create your own itinerary.
Iconic drives like Passo Sella, Passo Gardena, and Great Dolomites Road (Strada delle Dolomiti).
Considerations:

Parking can be limited in popular spots during peak seasons. Mountain roads can be steep and winding, so drive cautiously. In winter, snow chains or winter tires are often required.

2. By Bus

Public and private buses connect towns, villages, and popular attractions within the Dolomites.

Services:
Südtirol Mobil (South Tyrol): Covers towns like Bolzano, Val Gardena, and Alta Badia.
Dolomiti Bus: Operates in Belluno Province, serving areas like Cortina d'Ampezzo and Cadore.
Cortina Express: Links major hubs like Venice, Treviso, and Mestre with Dolomite towns.
Advantages:
Affordable and eco-friendly.
Ideal for traveling between towns without worrying about parking.
Considerations:
Schedules may be limited, especially in off-peak seasons.
Some remote locations may not have direct service.

3. By Train

While trains don't cover the heart of the Dolomites, they connect major towns on the outskirts.

Key Stations: Bolzano, Bressanone, and Brunico are the main hubs for train travelers.
Connecting Services: Use buses or taxis from train stations to reach mountain destinations.

4. By Cable Cars and Chairlifts

The Dolomites have an extensive network of lifts, primarily used for skiing in winter but also open in summer for hikers and sightseers.

Popular Areas with Lifts:
Val Gardena: Access to Seceda and Alpe di Siusi.
Cortina d'Ampezzo: Cable cars to Lagazuoi and Tofana di Mezzo.
Alta Badia: Great for reaching high-altitude hiking trails.
Advantages:
Stunning aerial views of the mountains.
Easy access to high-altitude trails and refuges.

5. By Bike

Cycling is a fantastic way to explore the Dolomites, especially for enthusiasts of road biking or mountain biking.

Options:
Rent bikes in towns like Cortina or Bolzano.
Try popular routes like the Sella Ronda Bike Day circuit.
Considerations:
Steep climbs and descents can be challenging.
E-bikes are widely available for those who want an easier ride.

6. By Taxi or Private Transfers

For convenience and direct routes, taxis and private transfers are widely available.

Best For:
Groups or families traveling with luggage.
Early morning or late-night trips when public transport is limited.

7. Guided Tours

Organized tours are a stress-free way to explore the region, especially for first-time visitors. Many tours include transportation, guides, and planned itineraries.

Options Include:
Hiking and biking tours.
Photography or cultural tours.

Tips for Getting Around

Plan Ahead: Check schedules for buses and lifts, especially in the off-season.
Use Transport Passes: Consider regional passes like the Südtirol Guest Pass, which offers unlimited travel on public transport.
Sustainability: The Dolomites encourage eco-friendly travel—use public transport or bike whenever possible.

With a mix of options, traveling within the Dolomites can be tailored to your preferences, whether you're seeking adventure or a relaxed exploration.

Packing Tips for Every Season in the Dolomites

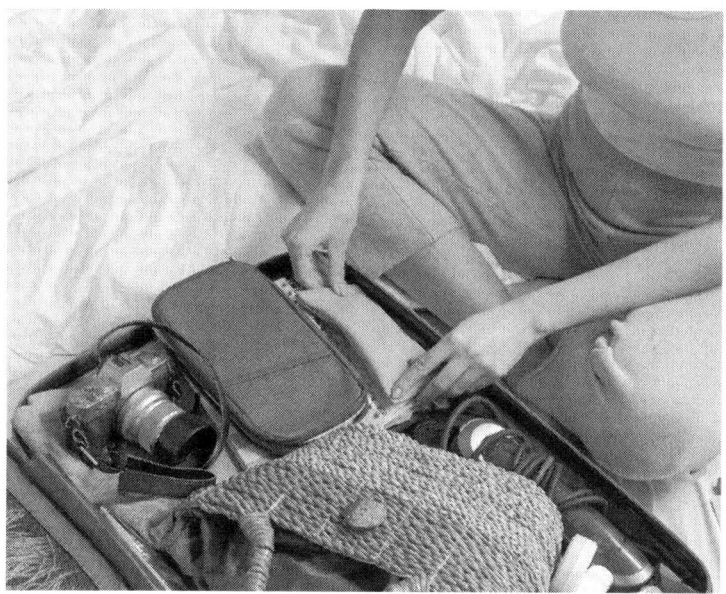

Packing smartly for the Dolomites ensures you're ready for all the activities and weather conditions the region has to offer. Here's a season-by-season guide to help you pack efficiently.

Spring (March to May)

Spring weather in the Dolomites can vary greatly, with lingering snow at higher altitudes and mild temperatures in the valleys.

Clothing:
Lightweight layers (base layers, fleece, and a waterproof jacket).

Warm hats and gloves for cooler mornings and evenings.
Comfortable hiking pants and moisture-wicking shirts.
Footwear:
Waterproof hiking boots (some trails may still be muddy or snowy).
Comfortable shoes for exploring villages.
Extras:
Trekking poles for stability on mixed terrain.
Sunglasses and sunscreen (spring sun can still be strong).

Summer (June to August)

Summer is ideal for outdoor adventures, with warm days and cooler nights. However, weather can change quickly in the mountains.

Clothing:
Breathable t-shirts, hiking shorts, and lightweight pants.
A fleece or down jacket for chilly evenings.
A waterproof, windproof jacket for sudden rainstorms.

Footwear:
Sturdy hiking boots with good grip for trails.
Sandals or comfortable walking shoes for casual outings.

Extras:
Daypack for carrying water, snacks, and essentials.
Reusable water bottle (many fountains provide fresh drinking water).
Hat and sunscreen for sun protection.

Autumn (September to November)

Autumn brings cooler temperatures and stunning foliage, making layering essential.

Clothing:

Insulated jackets and sweaters for crisp mornings.

Long-sleeve shirts and hiking pants.

Waterproof outerwear for potential rain.

Footwear:

Hiking boots suitable for wet or muddy conditions.

Warm socks for added comfort.

Extras:

Camera or phone for capturing fall colors.

Gloves and a scarf for late-autumn trips.

Winter (December to February)

Winter in the Dolomites is a snowy paradise, perfect for skiing and snowshoeing.

Clothing:

Thermal base layers, insulated jackets, and waterproof ski pants.

Wool hats, insulated gloves, and a neck gaiter or scarf.

Thick, moisture-wicking socks.

Footwear:

Snow boots or insulated hiking boots with good grip.

Ski boots (if you're bringing your own gear).

Extras:

Ski goggles and sunglasses to protect against snow glare.

Lip balm and heavy-duty moisturizer for dry winter air.

Hand warmers for long days outdoors.

General Packing Tips for All Seasons

Backpack: A sturdy daypack is essential for hikes and excursions.

First Aid Kit: Include band-aids, pain relievers, and blister care.

Travel Adapter: Italy uses Type C, F, or L plugs (230V).

Personal Items: ID, travel insurance, maps, and a small notebook for notes or journaling.

Snacks: High-energy snacks like trail mix or energy bars for longer outings.

Essential Apps and Resources for Exploring the Dolomites

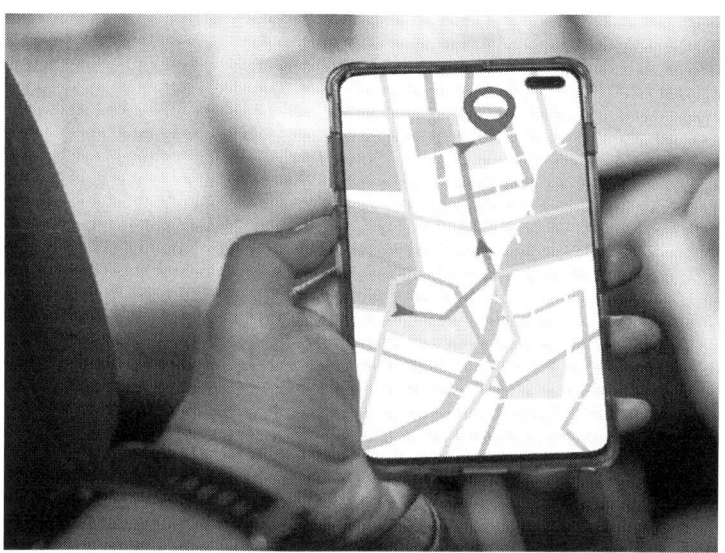

To make your trip to the Dolomites smooth and enjoyable, the right apps and resources can be incredibly helpful. From navigation and trail planning to weather updates and dining recommendations, here are the best tools to have at your fingertips.

1. Navigation and Transportation

Google Maps: Reliable for driving directions and finding restaurants, accommodations, and attractions.

Maps.me: Offline maps with detailed hiking and biking trails, perfect for areas with limited connectivity.

Südtirol Mobil: The go-to app for public transport schedules and routes in the South Tyrol region, including buses and trains.

Cortina Express: For shuttle services between key Dolomite towns and major airports like Venice and Treviso.

2. Hiking and Outdoor Activities

Komoot: Popular among hikers and cyclists, this app offers detailed trail maps, elevation profiles, and offline navigation.

AllTrails: Great for discovering the best hiking trails in the Dolomites, with user reviews and difficulty ratings.

Fatmap: A 3D map tool ideal for planning hiking, skiing, or climbing routes with high-level detail.

PeakVisor: Identify peaks and get information about mountains in real-time using augmented reality.

3. Weather Updates

Meteo Trentino: Provides accurate, localized weather forecasts for the Dolomites, including warnings for sudden changes in conditions.

Yr.no: Offers detailed, reliable weather updates, particularly useful for outdoor activities.

Windy: Perfect for checking wind conditions, which can be important for activities like paragliding or skiing.

4. Accommodation and Dining

Booking.com: Useful for finding accommodations ranging from budget-friendly B&Bs to luxurious chalets.

Airbnb: Offers unique stays, including traditional rifugios and private mountain lodges.

TripAdvisor: Find and review restaurants, attractions, and accommodations with traveler insights.

The Fork: Reserve tables at restaurants and discover dining options with reviews and discounts.

5. Skiing and Winter Sports

Dolomiti Superski App: Essential for skiers, with live updates on ski lift statuses, snow conditions, and ski pass information.

Skiline: Track your skiing statistics, including distances covered and altitude changes, and even view lift photos.

6. Language and Communication

Google Translate: Useful for quick translations between Italian, German, Ladin, and English. Download offline language packs for areas with poor signal.

SayHi: A voice translation app that can help you communicate with locals in real time.

7. Guides and Resources

Visit South Tyrol App: A comprehensive guide to the South Tyrol region, covering events, attractions, and practical tips.

Cortina Official App: Provides information about Cortina d'Ampezzo, including events, activities, and accommodations.

Rifugi del Trentino: Details mountain huts (rifugi) in the Trentino region, including booking options and availability.

8. Travel and Emergency Tools

WhatsApp: Widely used in Italy for messaging and staying in touch with hosts or guides.

112 Where Are U: A lifesaving app that connects you to local emergency services with your exact location

9. Photography and Stargazing

PhotoPills: Plan your shots with sun, moon, and Milky Way alignments, ideal for capturing the Dolomites' stunning vistas.

SkySafari: A stargazing app to enjoy clear mountain skies at night.

10. General Resources

Currency Converter: Stay updated on exchange rates if traveling from outside the Eurozone.

Rome2Rio: Plan multi-leg journeys, including trains, buses, and car rentals.

By using these apps and resources, you'll stay informed, organized, and prepared to make the most of your time in the Dolomites.

TOP DESTINATIONS IN THE DOLOMITES

Cortina d'Ampezzo: The Queen of the Dolomites

Cortina d'Ampezzo, often called the "Queen of the Dolomites," is a glamorous mountain town nestled in the Veneto region. Known for its breathtaking scenery, world-class skiing, and vibrant cultural scene, Cortina is a must-visit destination for travelers seeking both adventure and sophistication.

Why Visit Cortina d'Ampezzo?

Stunning Scenery: Surrounded by iconic peaks like Tofana di Rozes, Cristallo, and Sorapiss, Cortina offers panoramic views that captivate visitors year-round.

Skiing Paradise: As part of the Dolomiti Superski area, Cortina boasts over 120 kilometers of ski runs, with options for beginners and experts alike. The town hosted the 1956 Winter Olympics and will co-host the 2026 Winter Games.

Outdoor Adventures: Beyond skiing, Cortina is a hub for hiking, via ferrata climbing, mountain biking, and paragliding. The nearby Tre Cime di Lavaredo and Lago di Sorapiss are top attractions.

Chic Atmosphere: The town is a blend of luxury and charm, with high-end boutiques, stylish cafés, and fine dining restaurants that attract celebrities and discerning travelers.

Rich History and Culture: With roots in the Austro-Hungarian Empire, Cortina blends Italian and Tyrolean influences. Its unique culture is celebrated through festivals, architecture, and local cuisine.

Top Things to Do in Cortina d'Ampezzo

Hit the Slopes: Ski or snowboard at Tofana, Faloria, or Cristallo ski areas. Don't miss the Lagazuoi Cable Car for stunning views and challenging runs.

Explore the Dolomites: Take day trips to Tre Cime di Lavaredo, Cinque Torri, or the Great Dolomites Road for iconic hiking and sightseeing.

Visit Museums: Learn about World War I history at the Lagazuoi Open Air Museum or explore the Rinaldo Zardini Palaeontology Museum.

Indulge in Local Cuisine: Savor mountain specialties like casunziei (beet-filled pasta), polenta, and speck at traditional restaurants.

Shopping and Strolling: Wander along Corso Italia, Cortina's pedestrian-friendly main street, lined with designer boutiques, artisanal shops, and cafés.

Where to Stay

Cortina offers a range of accommodations, from luxury hotels like **Cristallo Resort & Spa** to charming mountain lodges and family-friendly apartments. Many options provide stunning views and easy access to ski lifts or hiking trails.

Getting There

By Car: Cortina is easily accessible via the A27 motorway from Venice or the A22 from Innsbruck.
By Public Transport: Cortina Express provides bus connections from Venice, Mestre, and Treviso.
By Train: The nearest train stations are in Dobbiaco or Calalzo di Cadore, with bus links to Cortina.

Best Time to Visit

Winter (December to March): For skiing, snowboarding, and winter sports.
Summer (June to September): Perfect for hiking, climbing, and exploring alpine lakes.

Cortina d'Ampezzo is the perfect blend of natural beauty, outdoor adventure, and alpine elegance, making it a top destination in the Dolomites.

Val Gardena: A Haven for Nature Lovers

Val Gardena, nestled in the heart of the Dolomites, is a picturesque valley that attracts visitors with its stunning landscapes, outdoor activities, and rich cultural heritage. Comprising three charming villages—Ortisei, Selva di Val Gardena, and Santa Cristina—Val Gardena is a paradise for those who love nature, adventure, and relaxation.

Why Visit Val Gardena?

Breathtaking Scenery: Surrounded by iconic peaks like Seceda, Sassolungo, and the Sella Group, Val Gardena offers jaw-dropping views year-round.

Outdoor Adventures: The valley is a gateway to hiking, skiing, and cycling routes, including access to the famous Dolomiti Superski area and the Sellaronda circuit.

Ladin Culture: Val Gardena is a cultural gem, with deep roots in Ladin traditions. Visitors can enjoy folk music, traditional crafts, and the Ladin language.

Family-Friendly Activities: From easy hiking trails to ski schools, Val Gardena offers plenty of activities for families with kids.
Charming Villages: The picturesque towns of Ortisei, Selva, and Santa Cristina each have unique attractions, from colorful streets to vibrant markets and cozy cafés.

Top Things to Do in Val Gardena

Hiking and Walking Trails:
Explore the dramatic ridges of Seceda or take a leisurely walk through Alpe di Siusi, Europe's largest alpine meadow.
Don't miss the Adolf Munkel Trail for breathtaking views of the Odle peaks.

Skiing and Snowboarding:
Val Gardena is part of the Dolomiti Superski network, offering over 500 kilometers of connected ski runs.
The Sellaronda circuit is a must for experienced skiers.

Cycling and Mountain Biking:
Cycle through scenic valleys or challenge yourself with the legendary Dolomites passes. The area is also great for e-biking.

Explore Ortisei:

Stroll through the vibrant town center, known for its colorful architecture, boutique shops, and art galleries.
Visit the Museum Gherdëina to learn about local history and Ladin culture.

Woodcarving Tradition:
Val Gardena is famous for its woodcarving artistry. Visit workshops and galleries to admire or purchase handcrafted wooden sculptures.

Relax in Nature:
Take a cable car ride to panoramic viewpoints like Dantercepies or Ciampinoi.
Enjoy the tranquility of Lago di Carezza or the wildflower-filled Alpe di Siusi.

Where to Stay

Val Gardena offers a wide range of accommodations:

Luxury Hotels: Hotel Adler Spa Resort in Ortisei provides top-tier wellness and stunning mountain views.
Charming Chalets: Stay in cozy lodges or apartments ideal for families and groups.
Mountain Refuges: Rifugios like Firenze Hut offer an authentic alpine experience.

Getting There

By Car: Access the valley via the A22 Brenner Motorway, exiting at Chiusa or Bolzano.
By Public Transport: Trains run to Bolzano or Bressanone, followed by a connecting bus to Val Gardena.
By Plane: Nearby airports include Innsbruck (120 km), Verona (190 km), and Venice (200 km).

Best Time to Visit

Summer (June to September): Perfect for hiking, cycling, and wildflower blooms.
Winter (December to March): Enjoy world-class skiing and snowboarding.

Val Gardena combines natural beauty, outdoor adventures, and cultural richness, making it a dream

Alpe di Siusi: Europe's Largest Alpine Meadow

Alpe di Siusi (Seiser Alm), Europe's largest high-altitude alpine meadow, is a serene and scenic destination in the Dolomites. Located in South Tyrol, this breathtaking plateau offers rolling green meadows, dramatic mountain backdrops, and a peaceful atmosphere that makes it a favorite for outdoor enthusiasts and those seeking relaxation.

Spectacular Scenery: The meadow is surrounded by iconic peaks like Sassolungo, Sassopiatto, and the Sciliar Massif, providing postcard-worthy views at every turn.

Outdoor Activities for All Ages: With a network of gentle trails, cycling paths, and ski slopes, Alpe di Siusi is perfect for families, beginners, and seasoned adventurers.

Peaceful Atmosphere: Unlike busier areas in the Dolomites, Alpe di Siusi offers a tranquil escape with fewer crowds and a relaxing vibe.

Culture and Cuisine: The area is steeped in Ladin traditions, with opportunities to enjoy hearty alpine dishes and experience local customs.

Top Things to Do in Alpe di Siusi

Hiking and Walking Trails:
Compaccio to Saltria: An easy walk offering panoramic views and ideal for families.

Hans and Paula Steger Trail: A scenic route that combines history and nature.

Sciliar Massif Hike: A more challenging trail with incredible viewpoints.
Cycling and E-Biking:
Explore the meadow on two wheels, with options for both leisurely rides and more challenging routes. E-bikes are available for rent to make the climbs easier.

Winter Sports:
Alpe di Siusi transforms into a snowy wonderland in winter, featuring cross-country skiing, downhill skiing, snowshoeing, and sledding.
The area is part of the Dolomiti Superski network, with ski schools and gentle slopes perfect for beginners.

Horseback Riding:
Explore the meadow on horseback for a unique way to enjoy its beauty. Guided tours are available for riders of all skill levels.

Relax and Unwind:
Enjoy the views from cozy alpine huts (rifugi) like Rifugio Molignon or Rifugio Bullaccia, where you can savor local dishes like speck, polenta, and Kaiserschmarrn.
Take a break at wellness resorts offering spa treatments with mountain views.

Where to Stay

Alpe di Siusi offers a range of accommodations:

Luxury Hotels: Alpina Dolomites Lodge provides high-end comfort with eco-friendly design and panoramic views.
Family-Friendly Resorts: Seiser Alm Urthaler is a great option for families with activities for kids.
Mountain Lodges: Stay at a rifugio for a more authentic alpine experience.

Getting There

By Cable Car: The Alpe di Siusi cable car connects the meadow to the town of Ortisei, making it easily accessible.

By Car: Cars are restricted in Alpe di Siusi during peak hours. Park in Compaccio and use shuttle buses or cable cars to explore further
.

By Public Transport: Regional buses run from Bolzano and other nearby towns to the cable car stations.

Best Time to Visit

Summer (June to September): Enjoy vibrant wildflowers, lush greenery, and endless hiking opportunities.
Winter (December to March): Perfect for skiing, sledding, and snowshoeing amidst snowy landscapes.

Alpe di Siusi is a haven of natural beauty, offering something for every traveler—whether you're seeking adventure, tranquility, or a connection with nature.

Tre Cime di Lavaredo: Iconic Peaks

Tre Cime di Lavaredo, or the Three Peaks of Lavaredo, is one of the most recognizable landmarks in the Dolomites. These three towering rock formations, located on the border of South Tyrol and Veneto, are a must-visit for hikers, climbers, and nature enthusiasts. Their striking beauty and accessibility make them an essential stop for anyone exploring the Dolomites.

Why Visit Tre Cime di Lavaredo?

Unmatched Scenery: The dramatic trio of peaks—Cima Grande, Cima Ovest, and Cima Piccola—are framed by rugged alpine landscapes, offering endless photo opportunities.

Hiking Paradise: Surrounded by well-maintained trails, Tre Cime is a haven for hikers of all skill levels, from short walks to more challenging treks.

Rich History: The area was a significant frontline during World War I, with historical remnants like tunnels and trenches to explore.

Wildlife and Flora: The region is home to diverse alpine plants and animals, adding to its natural charm.

Top Things to Do at Tre Cime di Lavaredo

Hike the Loop Trail:
The 10-kilometer trail around Tre Cime offers stunning views from every angle. It's a moderately easy hike with highlights like Rifugio Auronzo, Rifugio Lavaredo, and Rifugio Locatelli.

Time: 3–4 hours, depending on your pace.

Explore Historical Sites:
Visit remnants of World War I, including tunnels and observation points near the peaks, for a glimpse into the area's past.

Photography:
The peaks are especially photogenic at sunrise and sunset when the rock glows in shades of orange and pink.

Climbing:
Tre Cime is a world-renowned destination for rock climbers. Routes like the Spigolo Giallo on Cima Piccola offer thrilling challenges for experienced climbers.

Winter Activities:
In winter, the area transforms into a snowy wonderland, perfect for snowshoeing and ski touring.

Where to Stay

Mountain Huts (Rifugi): Stay at **Rifugio Auronzo** or **Rifugio Locatelli** for an authentic alpine experience with spectacular views.

Nearby Towns: Base yourself in **Cortina d'Ampezzo** or **Dobbiaco**, which offer a range of accommodations from luxury hotels to cozy B&Bs.

Getting There

By Car: Drive to Rifugio Auronzo via a toll road from Misurina. Parking is available, but it can fill up quickly in peak season.
By Bus: Shuttle buses run from Misurina to Rifugio Auronzo during the summer months.

On Foot: For a more immersive experience, hike up from Misurina or nearby villages.

Best Time to Visit

Summer (June to September): Ideal for hiking and clear views, with warmer temperatures and open rifugi.

Autumn (October): Offers quieter trails and stunning fall colors, though rifugi may close for the season.

Winter (December to March): A magical time for snow activities, but trails may be more challenging.

Tre Cime di Lavaredo's awe-inspiring peaks, combined with accessible trails and rich history, make it one of the Dolomites' most iconic and unforgettable destinations. Whether you're seeking adventure or serene beauty, this landmark is sure to leave a lasting impression.

Alta Badia: Gastronomy and Outdoor Fun

Alta Badia, a charming region in the Dolomites, is a favorite among foodies and outdoor enthusiasts alike. Located in South Tyrol, this area combines jaw-dropping alpine scenery, world-class skiing, and a rich Ladin cultural heritage. Known for its gourmet cuisine and vibrant outdoor activities, Alta Badia is a destination that satisfies both your appetite for adventure and fine dining.

Why Visit Alta Badia?

World-Class Gastronomy: Alta Badia is a hub for culinary excellence, boasting Michelin-starred restaurants, mountain rifugi offering traditional dishes, and events like "A Taste for Skiing."

Outdoor Adventures: With over 130 kilometers of ski slopes, endless hiking trails, and cycling routes, Alta Badia is perfect for active travelers.

Cultural Richness: The region's Ladin roots shine through in its language, architecture, and traditions.

Breathtaking Scenery: Framed by the Sella Group, Sassongher, and Lagazuoi peaks, Alta Badia offers some of the most stunning vistas in the Dolomites.

Top Things to Do in Alta Badia

Gourmet Experiences:

Taste for Skiing: This unique winter event combines skiing with gourmet food, as top chefs create dishes served at mountain huts.

Michelin Dining: Indulge in exceptional cuisine at restaurants like **St. Hubertus** in San Cassiano.

Local Specialties: Try dishes like *tutres* (savory pastries), *panicia* (barley soup), and apple strudel.

Skiing and Snowboarding:
Part of the Dolomiti Superski network, Alta Badia features slopes for all skill levels and easy access to the famous Sellaronda circuit.

Hiking and Cycling:
Hikes: Explore the Armentara Meadows, the Puez-Odle Nature Park, or the Pralongià Plateau for stunning landscapes.

Cycling: Test your endurance on the legendary Dolomite passes, such as Passo Gardena or Passo Campolongo, popular with road cyclists and during the annual Maratona dles Dolomites race.

Cultural Exploration:
Visit the Ladin Museum in San Martino in Badia to learn about the unique culture and history of the Ladin people.
Explore traditional alpine villages like Corvara, La Villa, and San Cassiano.

Wellness and Relaxation:
Many accommodations in Alta Badia offer wellness centers with saunas, pools, and spa treatments to unwind after a day of adventure.

Where to Stay

Luxury Hotels: Hotels like **Rosa Alpina** in San Cassiano provide upscale comfort with spa facilities and gourmet dining.

Family-Friendly Options: Residences and chalets in Corvara and La Villa cater to families with spacious apartments and kid-friendly amenities.

Mountain Rifugi: Stay at rifugi like Rifugio Lagazuoi for an authentic alpine experience with panoramic views

Getting There

By Car: Alta Badia is accessible via the A22 Brenner Motorway, exiting at Bressanone or Chiusa and continuing on mountain roads.
By Public Transport: Trains run to Brunico or Bolzano, with buses connecting to Alta Badia towns.
By Plane: Nearby airports include Innsbruck (120 km), Venice (200 km), and Verona (190 km)

Best Time to Visit

Summer (June to September): Perfect for hiking, cycling, and outdoor dining.

Winter (December to March): Ideal for skiing, snowboarding, and gourmet snow experiences.

Alta Badia is a destination where the love of nature and food come together. Whether you're carving through fresh powder, savoring Michelin-starred dishes, or enjoying a peaceful hike, this region offers unforgettable experiences for every traveler.

Bolzano and South Tyrol: Gateway to the Dolomites

Bolzano, the capital of South Tyrol, is the perfect starting point for exploring the Dolomites. Known for its blend of Italian and Tyrolean cultures, this vibrant city combines stunning landscapes, rich history, and urban comforts. South Tyrol, the surrounding region, is a haven for nature lovers, foodies, and history buffs, offering everything from scenic vineyards to alpine adventures.

Why Visit Bolzano and South Tyrol?

Cultural Fusion: Bolzano's unique mix of Italian and Germanic influences is reflected in its language, architecture, and cuisine.

Historical Significance: The region is home to landmarks like medieval castles, ancient churches, and Ötzi the Iceman, one of the world's oldest mummies.

Gateway to the Dolomites: Bolzano provides easy access to the Dolomites, with efficient transport links and guided tours to nearby attractions.

Scenic Beauty: South Tyrol offers lush vineyards, alpine meadows, and dramatic mountain peaks, creating a picturesque landscape year-round.

Top Things to Do in Bolzano and South Tyrol

Explore Bolzano's Old Town:

Stroll through Piazza Walther, the city's lively main square, surrounded by colorful buildings.

Visit the Gothic **Bolzano Cathedral** and its impressive bell tower.

Wander through **Via dei Portici**, a historic shopping street lined with arcades and boutiques.

Visit the South Tyrol Museum of Archaeology:
Learn about Ötzi the Iceman, a 5,300-year-old mummy discovered in the Alps, and explore exhibits on South Tyrol's ancient history.

Discover Nearby Castles:
Castel Roncolo (Runkelstein Castle): Famous for its medieval frescoes.

Maretsch Castle: Located in Bolzano, this picturesque castle is surrounded by vineyards.

Wine Tasting in the South Tyrolean Wine Road:
Explore the region's vineyards and sample local wines, including the famous Lagrein and Gewürztraminer varieties. Towns like Appiano and Caldaro are perfect for wine tours.

Outdoor Adventures:
Take a day trip to nearby Dolomite destinations like Alpe di Siusi, Val Gardena, or Tre Cime di Lavaredo.
Enjoy cycling, hiking, or skiing in South Tyrol's scenic landscapes.

Ride the Renon Cable Car:

Travel from Bolzano to the Renon Plateau for panoramic views, charming villages, and the famous Renon Earth Pyramids.

Where to Stay

Luxury Hotels: Parkhotel Laurin in Bolzano offers a mix of modern amenities and historical charm.

Boutique Accommodations: Stay in vineyard resorts or small family-run hotels in towns like Caldaro or Appiano.

Mountain Lodges: Rifugi in nearby Dolomite areas offer rustic, cozy stays for nature lovers.

Getting There

By Plane: Bolzano Airport (BZO) serves the region with limited flights. Larger airports like Innsbruck, Verona, or Venice are within a few hours by car.

By Train: Bolzano is well-connected by train to major Italian cities like Venice, Milan, and Verona.

By Car: The A22 Brenner Motorway passes through Bolzano, making it easily accessible by road.

Best Time to Visit

Spring (April to June): Perfect for exploring vineyards and enjoying mild weather.
Summer (July to September): Ideal for hiking and outdoor adventures in the surrounding mountains.

Winter (December to February): A great time for skiing and Christmas markets.

ACTIVITIES FOR EVERY SEASON

Spring: Wildflowers and Scenic Hikes

Spring in the Dolomites is a magical time as the snow melts, valleys bloom with vibrant wildflowers, and the region awakens with life. From picturesque hikes to charming villages, spring offers plenty of activities to enjoy the season's beauty.

Why Visit in Spring?

Blooming Meadows: Wildflowers blanket the alpine meadows, making it a dream for nature enthusiasts and photographers.

Pleasant Weather: Mild temperatures and longer days are ideal for exploring the outdoors.

Fewer Crowds: Spring is the shoulder season, so you can enjoy peaceful trails and uncrowded attractions.

Top Activities in Spring

Hiking Among Wildflowers:

Alpe di Siusi: Europe's largest alpine meadow comes alive with colorful blooms and panoramic views.
Pralongià Plateau: Gentle trails with breathtaking scenery and fields of crocus and primroses.

Adolf Munkel Trail: A moderate hike with stunning views of the Odle/Geisler peaks and wildflower-strewn paths.

Visit Scenic Lakes:
Lago di Braies: Known as the "Pearl of the Dolomites," this turquoise lake is especially tranquil in spring.

Lago di Carezza: The snowmelt enhances the lake's emerald hues, creating postcard-perfect reflections.

Cycling and E-Biking:
Many cycling routes reopen in spring, including gentle valley paths and challenging mountain climbs. Rent an e-bike for an easier ride through the Dolomites' stunning landscapes.

Explore Charming Villages:
Stroll through towns like Ortisei, Cortina d'Ampezzo, or Bolzano, where spring markets showcase local crafts and seasonal foods.

Wildlife Watching:
Spring is a great time to spot ibex, marmots, and chamois as they emerge from hibernation. Consider a guided nature walk for a deeper experience.

Photography:
Capture the vibrant colors of spring wildflowers, dramatic mountain backdrops, and peaceful lakes. Sunrise and sunset offer particularly magical lighting.

Practical Tips for Spring Visits

Layered Clothing: Weather can be unpredictable in spring, with warm days and chilly mornings or evenings. Bring a waterproof jacket for sudden rain showers.

Trail Conditions: Some higher-altitude trails may still have snow or be muddy from the thaw. Check conditions locally before heading out.

Opening Times: Some rifugi (mountain huts) and cable cars may not open until late spring, so plan accordingly.

Spring in the Dolomites offers a perfect mix of natural beauty, adventure, and tranquility. Whether you're hiking through wildflower meadows or exploring picturesque villages, this season is ideal for experiencing the Dolomites' softer, quieter side.

Summer: Via Ferrata, Mountain Biking, and Festivals

Summer in the Dolomites is the peak season for outdoor adventure, with warm temperatures, long days, and endless opportunities to explore the mountains. From thrilling via ferrata climbs to scenic bike trails and lively cultural festivals, summer offers something for every traveler.

Why Visit in Summer?

Ideal Weather: Warm days and cool evenings make it perfect for outdoor activities and high-altitude exploration.

Outdoor Adventures: The region's network of via ferrata routes, hiking trails, and cycling paths are fully accessible.

Festivals and Events: Summer is rich with cultural celebrations, music festivals, and traditional fairs.

Top Activities in Summer

Via Ferrata Adventures:
What It Is: Via ferrata are iron paths equipped with cables, ladders, and bridges, offering a thrilling way to explore the Dolomites' cliffs and peaks.
Popular Routes:
Via Ferrata Piz da Lech: A challenging climb with incredible views near Alta Badia.

Via Ferrata Brigata Tridentina: A classic route with a dramatic suspension bridge near Passo Gardena.

Via Ferrata Tomaselli: For experienced climbers seeking a technical challenge.

Tips: Rent or bring your own safety gear (harness, helmet, and carabiners) and consider a guide for added safety on challenging routes.

Mountain Biking and E-Biking:
Routes for All Levels:
Sellaronda MTB Tour: A legendary circuit around the Sella Group, accessible by bike or e-bike.

Alpe di Siusi Trails: Gentle routes with stunning meadow views, perfect for families.

Bike Rentals and Tours: Many towns, including Cortina d'Ampezzo and Val Gardena, offer bike rental services and guided tours for all skill levels.

Hiking and Trekking:
Explore trails like the **Tre Cime di Lavaredo Loop**, **Seceda Ridgeline**, or **Rosengarten Trails** for unforgettable scenery.

Multi-day treks, such as the **Alta Via 1**, offer immersive experiences with overnight stays in mountain rifugi.

Attend Festivals and Events:

Ladin Cultural Festivals: Celebrate the region's heritage with traditional music, dancing, and Ladin cuisine.

Maratona dles Dolomites: An iconic cycling event that attracts riders from around the globe.

Music Festivals: Enjoy performances in stunning settings, such as the Sounds of the Dolomites festival, which features open-air concerts in mountain meadows.

Rock Climbing:
The Dolomites are a climber's paradise, with routes ranging from beginner-friendly walls to technical multi-pitch climbs.
Areas like Cinque Torri and Marmolada offer some of the best climbing spots.

Photography and Stargazing:
Capture the Dolomites' stunning landscapes at sunrise or sunset.
Clear summer skies make the region perfect for stargazing, especially in remote areas.

Practical Tips for Summer Visits

Book Early: Accommodations and guided activities fill up quickly during summer, so reserve in advance.

Stay Hydrated: Carry plenty of water, as high-altitude trails can be dehydrating.

Start Early: Afternoon thunderstorms are common in summer, so begin hikes or climbs in the morning.

Wear Layers: Mornings can be cool, even in summer, so bring a light jacket or fleece.

Summer in the Dolomites is an adventurer's dream, offering endless ways to connect with nature and enjoy the region's vibrant culture. Whether you're scaling a via ferrata, cycling through alpine passes, or immersing yourself in local traditions, summer promises an unforgettable experience.

Autumn: Fall Colors and Quiet Trails

Autumn in the Dolomites is a serene and visually stunning season. As the summer crowds fade and the mountains transition to warm hues of gold, orange, and red, the region becomes an ideal destination for those seeking tranquility, breathtaking scenery, and outdoor adventures.

Why Visit in Autumn?

Spectacular Fall Colors: Larch trees, alpine meadows, and valleys turn vibrant shades, creating unforgettable landscapes.

Quiet Trails: With fewer visitors, you can enjoy peaceful hikes and attractions without the crowds.

Crisp, Refreshing Air: Cooler temperatures make outdoor activities even more enjoyable.

Top Activities in Autumn

Hiking Among Fall Foliage:
Lago di Braies: The lake mirrors the fiery colors of surrounding trees, offering postcard-perfect views.

Val di Funes: Trails like the Adolf Munkel Trail offer a mix of fall colors and panoramic views of the Odle peaks.
Seceda Ridgeline: Enjoy sweeping vistas of larch trees glowing in golden hues.

Alpe di Siusi: A leisurely walk through Europe's largest alpine meadow provides stunning autumn scenery.

Photography and Scenic Drives:

Passo Sella and Passo Gardena: These iconic mountain passes are especially photogenic in autumn.

Great Dolomites Road: Take a drive through valleys blanketed with fall colors and stop at scenic viewpoints.

Explore Quiet Villages:
Visit towns like Ortisei, Corvara, and San Candido for a blend of local charm, autumn markets, and cozy cafés serving seasonal treats like apple strudel and chestnut cakes.
Attend Harvest Festivals:

Autumn is the season of harvest, with festivals celebrating local produce, wine, and traditions. Events like the Törggelen in South Tyrol combine wine tasting with hearty dishes and cultural experiences.
Cycling and E-Biking:
Cooler weather and quieter trails make autumn a great time for cycling. Try routes like the Val Gardena Rail Trail or

Passo delle Erbe for a mix of fall foliage and mountain scenery.

Relax at a Spa or Wellness Center:
After a day outdoors, unwind in wellness resorts like those in Alta Badia or Val Gardena, where you can enjoy saunas, thermal pools, and massage treatments.

Wildlife Watching:

Autumn is a great time to spot animals like deer, chamois, and marmots preparing for winter. Consider joining a guided nature walk for a closer look at the region's wildlife.

Practical Tips for Autumn Visits

Layered Clothing: Morning and evening temperatures can be chilly, so pack warm layers and a waterproof jacket for unpredictable weather.

Check Trail Conditions: Some high-altitude trails may close for the season, so verify accessibility before heading out.
Fewer Rifugi Open: Many mountain huts close by late October, so plan hikes accordingly or base yourself in towns for dining options.

Best Autumn Experiences in the Dolomites

Watch the sun rise or set over the Dolomites, lighting up the autumn colors in a warm golden glow.

Visit Lago di Carezza, where the emerald waters contrast beautifully with the fall foliage.

Take leisurely walks through the Armentara Meadows in Alta Badia, one of the most scenic autumn spots in the region.

Autumn in the Dolomites offers a quieter, more intimate connection with the mountains. From vivid fall landscapes to peaceful trails and cultural festivities, it's the perfect time to experience the Dolomites in their most tranquil and colorful season.

Winter: Skiing, Snowboarding, and Christmas Markets

Winter in the Dolomites transforms the region into a snowy paradise. With world-class ski resorts, festive Christmas markets, and cozy alpine refuges, it's a season filled with adventure, charm, and holiday spirit. Whether you're carving down pristine slopes or enjoying a mug of mulled wine in a quaint village, winter in the Dolomites offers something magical for everyone.

Why Visit in Winter?

World-Class Winter Sports: The Dolomites are part of the Dolomiti Superski area, one of the largest ski networks in the world, with over 1,200 kilometers of slopes.

Festive Atmosphere: Christmas markets and holiday decorations add a warm, cheerful vibe to the season.

Snowy Scenery: Towering peaks and snow-blanketed valleys create breathtaking landscapes.

Top Activities in Winter

Skiing and Snowboarding:
Sellaronda Ski Circuit: A must-do for experienced skiers, this legendary route circles the Sella Group and connects multiple resorts.

Family-Friendly Areas: Val Gardena, Alta Badia, and Alpe di Siusi have gentle slopes and excellent ski schools for beginners and children.
Night Skiing: Experience the thrill of skiing under the stars at resorts like Obereggen.

Cross-Country Skiing and Snowshoeing:
Explore trails through scenic landscapes like the Alpe di Siusi or the Lavaze Plateau.

Guided snowshoeing tours are available for those who want to venture into peaceful, snow-covered forests and meadows.

Christmas Markets:
Bolzano: The largest Christmas market in Italy, featuring handcrafted gifts, festive foods, and twinkling lights.

Bressanone: Known for its magical setting and light shows projected onto the historic Bishop's Palace.

Brunico: A smaller, charming market with traditional South Tyrolean crafts and delicacies.

Sledding and Tobogganing:
Family-friendly sledding hills and dedicated toboggan runs are found in resorts like Obereggen and Val di Funes.

Relax in Mountain Refuges:

After a day on the slopes, unwind with a hearty meal or a warm drink at alpine huts (rifugi), many accessible by ski or foot.

Ice Skating:
Rinks in towns like Cortina d'Ampezzo or natural frozen lakes like Lago di Dobbiaco offer picturesque skating experiences.

Other Winter Highlights

Wellness and Spas: Treat yourself to a spa day in luxury resorts or thermal baths in towns like Alta Badia or Merano.

Horse-Drawn Sleigh Rides: Glide through snowy meadows in Alpe di Siusi for a fairytale-like experience.

Photography: Capture the Dolomites' iconic peaks dusted in snow, especially during sunrise or sunset when the mountains glow.

Practical Tips for Winter Visits

Layer Up: Pack thermal clothing, waterproof outerwear, insulated gloves, and a hat for staying warm in the cold.

Advance Bookings: Winter is a peak season, so book accommodations, ski passes, and rentals well in advance.

Snow Chains or Winter Tires: If driving, ensure your car is equipped for snowy conditions, especially on mountain roads.

Best Winter Experiences in the Dolomites

Ski the hidden gems of smaller resorts like Arabba or San Martino di Castrozza for fewer crowds.

Visit the Lagazuoi cable car and enjoy the breathtaking views from 2,800 meters.

Enjoy a traditional South Tyrolean Christmas dinner with dishes like roasted chestnuts, speck, and apple strudel.

Winter in the Dolomites offers a perfect mix of adventure and festivity. Whether you're hitting the slopes, exploring holiday markets, or simply enjoying the serene snow-covered landscapes, this season is full of unforgettable experiences.

OUTDOOR ADVENTURES

Best Hiking Trails for All Skill Levels

of the most spectacular hiking experiences in the world, with trails suitable for beginners, families, and experienced adventurers. Whether you're looking for a gentle stroll through alpine meadows or a challenging trek with dramatic mountain views, there's a trail for everyone.

For Beginners and Families

Alpe di Siusi (Seiser Alm):
Overview: Europe's largest alpine meadow offers easy, flat trails with stunning views of Sassolungo and Sciliar peaks.

Distance: 5–10 km options.
Highlights: Wildflowers in summer, golden larches in autumn, and family-friendly huts serving traditional Ladin dishes.

The Dolomites offer some

Val di Funes – Adolf Munkel Trail:
Overview: A scenic loop trail beneath the dramatic Odle/Geisler peaks.
Distance: 8 km (3–4 hours).

Highlights: Iconic Dolomite views, lush forests, and picturesque meadows.

Lago di Braies (Pragser Wildsee):
Overview: A flat, easy path around the turquoise waters of this famous lake.
Distance: 3.5 km (1 hour).
Highlights: Stunning reflections of the surrounding peaks, perfect for photography.

Moderate Trails

Seceda Ridgeline:
Overview: A moderate hike offering panoramic views of the Dolomites' jagged peaks and sweeping valleys.
Distance: 6–10 km (4–5 hours).
Highlights: Iconic photo spots and options to start or end via the Ortisei cable car.

Cinque Torri:
Overview: A loop trail showcasing the famous rock formations of the Cinque Torri (Five Towers).
Distance: 9 km (3–4 hours).
Highlights: World War I trenches, rifugi, and stunning rock spires.

Tre Cime di Lavaredo Loop:
Overview: One of the most famous Dolomite hikes, circling the iconic Three Peaks.
Distance: 10 km (3–4 hours).

Highlights: Sweeping views, rifugi stops, and a mix of gentle and rocky paths.

Challenging Trails

Alta Via 1 – Stage Hikes:
Overview: This legendary long-distance trail runs north to south through the Dolomites, with stages suitable for day hikes.
Distance: Variable; popular sections are 8–15 km per day.
Highlights: Towering peaks, tranquil alpine lakes, and overnight stays in rifugi.

Rosengarten Group – Vajolet Towers:
Overview: A challenging hike to one of the most dramatic rock formations in the Dolomites.

Distance: 12 km (5–6 hours).
Highlights: The famous Vajolet Towers, high-altitude views, and alpine flora.

Marmolada Glacier Hike:
Overview: A strenuous hike offering close-up views of the Dolomites' highest peak and its glacier.
Distance: 12–15 km (6–7 hours).
Highlights: Stunning vistas, historical World War I landmarks, and the option to combine with cable car rides.

Tips for Hiking in the Dolomites

Plan Ahead: Check weather conditions and trail updates before heading out.

Gear Up: Wear sturdy hiking boots, dress in layers, and carry essentials like water, snacks, and a map or GPS.

Timing Matters: Start early to avoid afternoon thunderstorms, especially in summer.

Stay Safe: Some trails may require basic climbing skills or familiarity with exposed paths; research the difficulty level in advance.

Rifugi Stops: Many trails include mountain huts where you can enjoy a meal, rest, or even stay overnight.

Whether you're strolling around scenic lakes or tackling high-altitude routes, the Dolomites' hiking trails showcase the region's stunning natural beauty and variety, ensuring unforgettable adventures for all skill levels.

Via Ferrata: A Beginner's Guide

Via ferrata, or "iron paths," are protected climbing routes featuring steel cables, ladders, and bridges that allow hikers to explore dramatic mountain terrain with added safety. Originating in the Dolomites during World War I, via ferrata is now a popular activity for adventurers of all levels.

This guide will help beginners understand what to expect, how to prepare, and which routes to start with in the Dolomites.

What is Via Ferrata?

Via ferrata routes are fixed climbing paths that use anchored cables, rungs, and bridges to assist climbers in scaling rock faces and traversing exposed areas. They provide an exciting way to experience the Dolomites' vertical landscapes, combining elements of hiking and climbing without requiring advanced technical skills

Essential Gear for Via Ferrata

Helmet: Protects against falling rocks or accidental bumps on the route.
Harness: Secures you to the via ferrata cable for safety.

Via Ferrata Kit: Includes a lanyard with carabiners and energy absorbers to catch you in case of a fall.

Sturdy Footwear: Approach shoes or hiking boots with good grip are ideal.

Gloves: Lightweight gloves protect your hands while gripping cables.

Backpack: A small pack for water, snacks, and a jacket.

Tips for Beginners

Start Easy: Choose beginner-friendly routes to build confidence and get used to the gear.

Practice Clipping: Learn how to safely clip and unclip your carabiners from the cable.

Go with a Guide: If it's your first time, consider hiring a guide to ensure safety and proper technique.

Plan Ahead: Research the route's difficulty and make sure it matches your fitness level. Routes are graded from easy (A) to very difficult (E).

Check Conditions: Avoid via ferrata in bad weather; wet or icy conditions make the routes dangerous.

Beginner-Friendly Via Ferrata Routes in the Dolomites

Via Ferrata Piz da Lech (Alta Badia):
Grade: B (easy to moderate).

Highlights: A short, scenic route with stunning views of the Sella Group. Perfect for beginners with some adventurous spirit.

Via Ferrata Col dei Bos (Cortina d'Ampezzo):
Grade: B (easy to moderate).

Highlights: Combines moderate climbing with stunning vistas and historical World War I trenches.

Via Ferrata Gran Cir (Val Gardena):

Grade: A/B (easy).

Highlights: A beginner-friendly route with minimal exposure and spectacular summit views.
Sentiero dei Kaiserjäger (Lagazuoi):

Grade: A/B (easy).
Highlights: A historically significant route with breathtaking views and a mix of hiking and climbing.

Via Ferrata Averau (Cinque Torri):
Grade: A/B (easy).

Highlights: A short, enjoyable route with panoramic views, perfect for first-timers.

What to Expect on Your First Via Ferrata

Physical Effort: While not as demanding as traditional climbing, via ferrata requires basic fitness and comfort with heights.

Exposure: Many routes feature narrow ledges and vertical climbs, so take it slow if you're new to these conditions.

Supportive Environment: Most beginner routes are well-maintained and offer ample footholds and handholds for easier climbing.

Safety Tips

Inspect Your Gear: Make sure your helmet good condition before starting.

Clip Properly: Always stay clipped to the cable, transitioning one carabiner at a time.

Keep Distance: Maintain space between climbers to avoid overcrowding on the route.

Stay Calm: Take breaks if needed and focus on each step rather than looking down.

When to Go

The best time for via ferrata in the Dolomites is from late spring to early autumn (June to September), when weather conditions are most favorable, and snow has melted from the higher routes.

Via ferrata is an exhilarating way to experience the Dolomites' dramatic peaks and cliffs. With the right preparation, gear, and guidance, beginners can safely enjoy this unforgettable adventure.

Paragliding and Other Unique Activities

The Dolomites' breathtaking landscapes and dramatic peaks make it a perfect playground for thrilling and one-of-a-kind activities. From soaring through the skies while paragliding to exploring hidden corners of the region, here's a guide to the most unique experiences in the Dolomites.

Paragliding in the Dolomites

Why It's Amazing: Paragliding offers a bird's-eye view of the Dolomites, with its towering peaks, lush valleys, and shimmering lakes. It's an adrenaline-packed way to take in the region's unparalleled beauty.

Best Launch Sites:

Seceda (Val Gardena): Soar above the iconic ridgeline with sweeping views of the Odle Peaks.

Alpe di Siusi: Enjoy a gentle glide over Europe's largest alpine meadow.

Col Rodella (Val di Fassa): Known as one of the best paragliding spots in the Dolomites, with stunning views of the Sella Group.

How to Try It:

Tandem flights are available for beginners, no experience needed. Professional pilots guide you through takeoff, flight, and landing.

Popular providers include Fly2Fun (Val Gardena) and Fassa Fly (Val di Fassa).

Best Time: Summer and early autumn (June to October) offer the most stable weather conditions for flying.

2. Hot Air Balloon Rides

Why It's Unique: Float gently above the Dolomites, enjoying panoramic views and a tranquil experience. Perfect for those who prefer a less extreme adventure than paragliding.

Best Operators: Companies like Balloon Team Italia offer flights near Cortina d'Ampezzo and Val Pusteria.

Highlights: Sunrise flights provide magical lighting over snow-capped peaks and alpine valleys.

3. Climbing and Bouldering

Why It's Special: The Dolomites are a climber's paradise, offering everything from beginner-friendly climbing walls to challenging multi-pitch routes.

Top Spots:
Cinque Torri near Cortina d'Ampezzo.
Marmolada, for those seeking technical climbs.
Sella Pass, with routes for all skill levels.

Guided Tours: Local guides can introduce you to climbing in the region and ensure safety on more challenging routes.

4. Canyoning

Why It's Thrilling: Explore narrow gorges, rappel down waterfalls, and wade through streams in this adventurous water activity.

Best Locations:
Rio Nero Canyon (near Madonna di Campiglio): Perfect for beginners and families.

Torrente Grigno (Valsugana): A more challenging canyoning route.
What's Involved: Guided tours provide all necessary equipment, including wetsuits, harnesses, and helmets.

5. Helicopter Tours

Why It's Memorable: Get an unparalleled view of the Dolomites' dramatic landscapes, including the Tre Cime di Lavaredo, Marmolada Glacier, and Sella Massif.

Best Providers: Companies like Elico or HeliUnion offer scenic flights from Cortina d'Ampezzo or Bolzano.

Duration: Flights range from 15 minutes to over an hour, depending on the package.

6. Wildlife Safaris

Why It's Unique: Spot wildlife like ibex, chamois, golden eagles, and marmots in their natural habitat.

Best Locations:
Puez-Odle Nature Park.
Fanes-Sennes-Braies Nature Park.

Guided Tours: Join a local expert who can provide insights into the region's flora and fauna.

7. Explore Ice Caves (Winter Only)

Why It's Magical: In winter, frozen waterfalls and underground ice formations create a surreal experience.

Best Locations:
Marmolada Glacier Ice Cave.
Serrai di Sottoguda Gorge, near Arabba.

8. Traditional Ladin Cooking Classes

Why It's Special: Learn to prepare local dishes like *tutres* (savory pastries) or *canederli* (dumplings) with guidance from locals.
Where to Try It: Many family-run farms and small hotels in Alta Badia and Val Gardena offer cooking workshops.

9. Stargazing in Remote Areas

Why It's Stunning: The Dolomites' remote locations and high altitudes make them perfect for clear, star-filled skies.

Best Spots:
Passo Sella.
Lago di Misurina.
Tips: Visit during a new moon for optimal stargazing conditions.

10. E-Bike Adventures

Why It's Fun: Explore scenic trails and tackle mountain passes with less effort using an electric bike.

Top Trails:
The Sellaronda MTB Tour.
Val Pusteria cycling path.

Rental Options: E-bikes are widely available in towns like Cortina d'Ampezzo and Alta Badia.

Tips for Unique Activities

Book Ahead: Activities like paragliding, hot air balloon rides, and helicopter tours often fill up quickly during peak seasons.

Dress Appropriately: Wear weather-appropriate clothing and sturdy footwear for outdoor adventures.

Check Conditions: Weather can be unpredictable, so confirm your activity closer to the date

The Dolomites offer endless ways to connect with nature and enjoy unforgettable experiences. From soaring above the peaks to exploring hidden gorges and caves, these unique activities will add adventure and excitement to your trip.

DOLOMITES FOR FAMILIES

Kid-Friendly Hikes and Activities

The Dolomites are a fantastic destination for families, offering a range of easy hikes, fun activities, and scenic attractions that kids and adults will love. Whether you're exploring gentle trails, visiting adventure parks, or enjoying interactive museums, the Dolomites ensure a family-friendly experience filled with adventure and bonding time.

Why the Dolomites Are Great for Families

Accessible Trails: Many hikes are easy and stroller-friendly, making them suitable for young children.

Outdoor Adventure: Kids can enjoy nature playgrounds, alpine meadows, and fun activities like sledding or zip-lining.

Cultural Experiences: Interactive museums and traditional farms provide educational opportunities

Top Kid-Friendly Hikes

Alpe di Siusi (Seiser Alm):

Overview: A flat, stroller-friendly trail through Europe's largest alpine meadow.
Distance: Customizable (short loops or longer routes).
Highlights: Stunning views, wildflowers, and friendly farm animals.
Extras: Stop at family-friendly rifugi for snacks and drinks.

Val di Funes – St. Magdalena Circuit:

Overview: A gentle loop trail with breathtaking views of the Odle/Geisler peaks.
Distance: 5 km (2 hours).
Highlights: Picture-perfect scenery and plenty of spots for a family picnic.

Prato Piazza (Plätzwiese):

Overview: A wide, easy path in a peaceful alpine plateau.
Distance: 4–6 km options.
Highlights: Stunning mountain views, safe for kids to explore.

Tre Cime di Lavaredo – Easy Section:

Overview: Start from Rifugio Auronzo and walk the first section of the Tre Cime trail.
Distance: 2–3 km (1 hour).
Highlights: Iconic views of the Three Peaks, accessible for little adventurers.

Lake Walks (Lago di Braies or Lago di Carezza):

Overview: Flat, easy walks around these stunning alpine lakes.
Distance: 3–4 km (1–1.5 hours).
Highlights: Crystal-clear water, photo opportunities, and fun spots for kids to play.

Kid-Friendly Activities

Adventure Parks:
Col de Flam Adventure Park (Val Gardena): Features zip lines, rope courses, and a small petting zoo.
Dolomiti Adventure Park (Forni di Sopra): Perfect for older kids, with climbing courses tailored to different skill levels.

Animal Encounters:
Visit local farms like **Unterlanzin Hof (Ortisei)**, where kids can meet cows, goats, and chickens.
Animal Park Dobbiaco: A small wildlife park featuring deer, goats, and other alpine animals.

Alpine Coasters:
Funbob Alpine Coaster (Baranci): A thrilling, family-friendly toboggan ride through scenic mountain landscapes.

Interactive Museums:
Messner Mountain Museum (Various Locations): Explore exhibits about mountain culture and history, with kid-friendly displays.
South Tyrol Museum of Archaeology (Bolzano): Kids will love learning about Ötzi the Iceman.

Nature Playgrounds:
Val di Funes Adventure Trail: Combines an easy walk with play areas and educational displays about the local environment.

Piz Sorega Movimënt Park (Alta Badia): A mountaintop playground with slides, climbing structures, and even a mini-golf course.

Sledding and Snow Play (Winter):
In winter, many ski resorts like Alpe di Siusi or Cortina d'Ampezzo offer dedicated sledding areas and snow parks for families.

Tips for Family Travel in the Dolomites

Stay in Family-Friendly Accommodations: Look for hotels or chalets with playgrounds, kids' clubs, or babysitting services.

Plan Breaks: Include plenty of rest stops for snacks and playtime, especially on hikes.

Pack Smart: Bring layers, sunscreen, hats, and plenty of water for outdoor adventures.

Choose Accessible Locations: Base yourself in areas like Ortisei, Cortina, or Alta Badia, which are well-equipped for families.

Best Seasons for Families

Summer (June to September): Perfect for hikes, nature playgrounds, and outdoor exploration.
Winter (December to February): Great for skiing, sledding, and cozy evenings in mountain lodges.

The Dolomites provide the perfect mix of adventure, education, and fun for families. Whether hiking among stunning peaks or enjoying interactive activities, it's a destination that creates lasting memories for kids and parents alike.

Best Ski Areas for Children

The Dolomites are an excellent destination for family skiing, offering child-friendly slopes, top-notch ski schools, and plenty of fun activities for kids. Whether your little ones are beginners or already comfortable on skis, these ski areas provide a safe and enjoyable environment for families.

Why the Dolomites Are Great for Kids

Gentle Slopes: Many resorts have wide, easy slopes ideal for young learners.

Ski Schools: Highly-rated instructors specialize in teaching children of all ages.

Fun Zones: Snow parks, magic carpets, and themed areas keep kids entertained.

Family Facilities: Resorts offer amenities like childcare services, play areas, and family-friendly accommodations

Top Ski Areas for Children

Alpe di Siusi (Seiser Alm):
Why It's Great for Kids:
Gentle slopes and beginner-friendly ski runs.
Excellent ski schools with experienced instructors.
Snow parks with fun features like tunnels, slides, and magic carpets.

Extras: Families can enjoy sledding and horse-drawn sleigh rides.

Bonus: A quieter atmosphere makes it less intimidating for young skiers.

Val Gardena:

Why It's Great for Kids:

Wide nursery slopes and dedicated children's areas, such as the "Snowman Park."

Ski schools like Scuola Sci Selva specialize in teaching children.

Extras: Play areas and kid-friendly après-ski activities in Ortisei and Selva.
Bonus: Easy access to Alpe di Siusi via cable car for more family options.

Alta Badia:

Why It's Great for Kids:

Gentle ski runs and multiple baby lifts.

Kids' Snow Park in San Cassiano offers fun obstacles and a safe learning environment.

Extras: Movimënt Parks provide snow playgrounds with interactive features and ski trails designed for families.

Bonus: Family-friendly hotels with childcare options.

Kronplatz (Plan de Corones):

Why It's Great for Kids:

Excellent beginner slopes and modern lifts with safety features for children.

Ski schools offering group lessons and private sessions for kids.

Extras: The "Croniworld" snow park is tailored for kids, with magic carpets and mascots.

Bonus: Sledding areas and nearby family-friendly accommodations.

Cortina d'Ampezzo:

Why It's Great for Kids:
Beginner slopes at Socrepes and Mietres designed for children.

Experienced ski schools like Scuola Sci Cortina offering child-friendly lessons.

Extras: Snow play areas and sledding hills.

Bonus: Parents can enjoy stunning views and more advanced runs while kids learn.

Val di Fassa:

Why It's Great for Kids:

Beginner areas like Buffaure and Canazei offer easy slopes.

The "Kinderland" in Campitello di Fassa is a dedicated kids' zone with play features and beginner ski tracks.
Extras: Fun après-ski activities like ice skating and snow tubing.

Arabba:

Why It's Great for Kids:

Quiet slopes and beginner-friendly runs in a less crowded resort.

Child-focused ski schools with patient instructors.

Extras: Nearby family-friendly trails for winter walks.

Features to Look for in Kid-Friendly Ski Areas

Ski Schools: Choose areas with well-reviewed children's ski schools.

Magic Carpets: Easier for young kids than traditional ski lifts.

Snow Parks: Fun zones with tunnels, small jumps, and play equipment.

Proximity to Accommodations: Short distances from slopes to lodging make everything easier for families.

Tips for Family Skiing

Book Lessons Early: Ski schools fill up quickly during peak seasons.

Dress in Layers: Keep kids warm and comfortable with proper ski gear.

Take Breaks: Plan for rest stops at mountain huts (rifugi) for hot chocolate and snacks.

Safety First: Make sure kids wear helmets and use beginner-friendly slopes.

Best Time to Ski with Kids

December to March: Offers great snow conditions, and many resorts host family-friendly holiday events and activities.

The Dolomites cater wonderfully to families, making skiing with kids a fun and memorable experience. With gentle slopes, engaging activities, and expert ski schools, these ski areas ensure that little ones have as much fun as the grown-ups.

Family-Friendly Accommodations and Restaurants

The Dolomites offer a variety of family-friendly accommodations and restaurants that cater to the needs of parents and children alike. From hotels with dedicated kids' areas to restaurants serving hearty dishes that everyone will love, families will feel right at home in this alpine wonderland.

Family-Friendly Accommodations

Alpina Dolomites Lodge (Alpe di Siusi):
Why It's Great: Offers spacious family suites, kids' programs, and stunning views of the Seiser Alm.
Extras: An indoor pool, wellness center, and guided family hikes in summer.

Cavallino Bianco Family Spa Grand Hotel (Ortisei):

Why It's Great: Specifically designed for families, with kids' clubs, babysitting services, and activities for all ages.

Extras: A dedicated spa for children and a water park.

Hotel Piz Seteur (Selva di Val Gardena):

Why It's Great: Located near beginner-friendly ski slopes and hiking trails.

Extras: A playroom and outdoor playground make it perfect for younger kids.

Family Hotel Biancaneve (Santa Cristina):

Why It's Great: Offers family suites, a kids' play area, and an indoor pool.

Extras: Ski-in/ski-out access and child-friendly ski lessons nearby.

Sporthotel Panorama (Corvara, Alta Badia):

Why It's Great: Family-friendly rooms, organized activities for kids, and easy access to ski lifts and hiking trails.

Extras: On-site childcare and a wellness area for parents.

Hotel Dolomitenblick (Val Pusteria):

Why It's Great: A relaxed, family-run hotel with spacious rooms and a cozy atmosphere.

Extras: Large gardens, seasonal activities, and kid-friendly dining options.

Residence Adler (Alpe di Siusi):

Why It's Great: Family apartments with kitchens for flexible dining and access to outdoor adventures.

Extras: Close proximity to hiking trails and playgrounds.

Family-Friendly Restaurants

Rifugio Zallinger (Alpe di Siusi):
Why It's Great: A cozy mountain hut with a warm atmosphere and stunning views.
Kid Appeal: The menu includes hearty dishes like pasta and schnitzel that kids love.

Adlerkeller (Ortisei):
Why It's Great: A welcoming spot offering both Italian and Tyrolean specialties.
Kid Appeal: Spacious seating and familiar dishes like pizza and spaghetti.

Rifugio Scoiattoli (Cinque Torri):
Why It's Great: Located near hiking trails, with a sunny terrace and breathtaking mountain views.
Kid Appeal: Fun for kids to explore the surroundings while parents relax.

Pizzeria Tiroler Stube (Cortina d'Ampezzo):
Why It's Great: Combines a traditional alpine setting with family-friendly service.
Kid Appeal: Delicious wood-fired pizzas and a welcoming atmosphere.

Ristorante Da Peppa (Selva di Val Gardena):
Why It's Great: Casual dining with a mix of Italian and Ladin cuisine.
Kid Appeal: Simple options like pasta, pizza, and desserts kids will enjoy.

Rifugio Fodara Vedla (Fanes-Sennes-Braies Nature Park):
Why It's Great: Located in a serene alpine setting with hearty food and a kids' menu.

Kid Appeal: A small playground and plenty of open space for children to explore.

Baita Panorama (Alta Badia):
Why It's Great: Offers panoramic views, warm hospitality, and delicious alpine dishes.

Kid Appeal: Outdoor seating with space for kids to roam and a simple, tasty menu.

What to Look for in Family-Friendly Accommodations and Restaurants

Accommodations:
Spacious family rooms or apartments.
Amenities like playrooms, pools, or babysitting services.
Proximity to family-friendly activities like gentle ski slopes or hiking trails.

Restaurants:
Menus with kid-friendly options like pasta, pizza, or schnitzel.
Comfortable, casual environments where children are welcome.
Scenic locations that allow kids to play while parents enjoy a relaxed meal.

Tips for Families

Make Reservations: Popular family-friendly accommodations and restaurants can book up quickly, especially during peak seasons.

Check Amenities: Look for facilities like high chairs, kids' menus, and play areas to make dining and staying more enjoyable.

Plan Flexibly: Choose accommodations with nearby dining options or kitchens for convenience.

The Dolomites' family-friendly accommodations and restaurants ensure a comfortable and enjoyable experience for parents and kids alike. With thoughtful amenities and welcoming atmospheres, you'll have everything you need to create cherished family memories.

Kid-Friendly Hikes and Activities

The Dolomites are a fantastic destination for families, offering a range of easy hikes, fun activities, and scenic attractions that kids and adults will love. Whether you're exploring gentle trails, visiting adventure parks, or enjoying interactive museums, the Dolomites ensure a family-friendly experience filled with adventure and bonding time.

Why the Dolomites Are Great for Families

Accessible Trails: Many hikes are easy and stroller-friendly, making them suitable for young children.

Outdoor Adventure: Kids can enjoy nature playgrounds, alpine meadows, and fun activities like sledding or zip-lining.

Cultural Experiences: Interactive museums and traditional farms provide educational opportunities.

Top Kid-Friendly Hikes

Alpe di Siusi (Seiser Alm):

Overview: A flat, stroller-friendly trail through Europe's largest alpine meadow.

Distance: Customizable (short loops or longer routes).

Highlights: Stunning views, wildflowers, and friendly farm animals.
Extras: Stop at family-friendly rifugi for snacks and drinks.

Val di Funes – St. Magdalena Circuit:

Overview: A gentle loop trail with breathtaking views of the Odle/Geisler peaks.

Distance: 5 km (2 hours).

Highlights: Picture-perfect scenery and plenty of spots for a family picnic.

Prato Piazza (Plätzwiese):Overview: A wide, easy path in a peaceful alpine plateau.
Distance: 4–6 km options.

Highlights: Stunning mountain views, safe for kids to explore.
Tre Cime di Lavaredo – Easy Section:

Overview: Start from Rifugio Auronzo and walk the first section of the Tre Cime trail.
Distance: 2–3 km (1 hour).

Highlights: Iconic views of the Three Peaks, accessible for little adventurers.

Lake Walks (Lago di Braies or Lago di Carezza):

Overview: Flat, easy walks around these stunning alpine lakes.
Distance: 3–4 km (1–1.5 hours).

Highlights: Crystal-clear water, photo opportunities, and fun spots for kids to play.

Kid-Friendly Activities

Adventure Parks:

Col de Flam Adventure Park (Val Gardena): Features zip lines, rope courses, and a small petting zoo.

Dolomiti Adventure Park (Forni di Sopra): Perfect for older kids, with climbing courses tailored to different skill levels.

Animal Encounters:

Visit local farms like **Unterlanzin Hof (Ortisei)**, where kids can meet cows, goats, and chickens.

Animal Park Dobbiaco: A small wildlife park featuring deer, goats, and other alpine animals.

Alpine Coasters:

Funbob Alpine Coaster (Baranci): A thrilling, family-friendly toboggan ride through scenic mountain landscapes.

Interactive Museums:

Messner Mountain Museum (Various Locations): Explore exhibits about mountain culture and history, with kid-friendly displays.

South Tyrol Museum of Archaeology (Bolzano): Kids will love learning about Ötzi the Iceman.

Nature Playgrounds:

Val di Funes Adventure Trail: Combines an easy walk with play areas and educational displays about the local environment.

Piz Sorega Movimënt Park (Alta Badia): A mountaintop playground with slides, climbing structures, and even a mini-golf course.

Sledding and Snow Play (Winter):

In winter, many ski resorts like Alpe di Siusi or Cortina d'Ampezzo offer dedicated sledding areas and snow parks for families.

Tips for Family Travel in the Dolomites

Stay in Family-Friendly Accommodations: Look for hotels or chalets with playgrounds, kids' clubs, or babysitting services.

Plan Breaks: Include plenty of rest stops for snacks and playtime, especially on hikes.

Pack Smart: Bring layers, sunscreen, hats, and plenty of water for outdoor adventures.

Choose Accessible Locations: Base yourself in areas like Ortisei, Cortina, or Alta Badia, which are well-equipped for families.

Best Seasons for Families

Summer (June to September): Perfect for hikes, nature playgrounds, and outdoor exploration.

Winter (December to February): Great for skiing, sledding, and cozy evenings in mountain lodges.

The Dolomites provide the perfect mix of adventure, education, and fun for families. Whether hiking among stunning peaks or enjoying interactive activities, it's a

FOOD AND DRINK IN THE DOLOMITES

Traditional Dishes to Try

The Dolomites' cuisine is a delightful fusion of Italian, Tyrolean, and Ladin influences, reflecting the region's rich history and mountainous terrain. From hearty comfort foods to delicate desserts, the Dolomites offer a variety of traditional dishes that are a must-try for any food lover.

Starters and Soups

Speck (Cured Ham):
What It Is: A lightly smoked, dry-cured ham, often served thinly sliced.

How to Enjoy It: On its own, with bread, or as part of an antipasto platter with cheese.
Barley Soup (Panicia):

What It Is: A warming soup made with barley, vegetables, and smoked pork.
When to Try It: Perfect for a chilly day in a mountain rifugio.

Hay Soup:
What It Is: A creamy soup infused with mountain hay, served with crispy bread.

Where to Find It: Popular in Alpe di Siusi and nearby areas.

Main Courses

Canederli (Dumplings):
What It Is: Bread dumplings mixed with speck, spinach, or cheese, served in broth or with butter and sage.
Why You'll Love It: Hearty, flavorful, and a staple of Dolomite cuisine.

Schlutzkrapfen (Stuffed Pasta):
What It Is: Ravioli-like pasta filled with spinach and ricotta, topped with butter and Parmesan.
A Local Favorite: Often made with whole-grain flour for a nutty flavor.

Polenta:
What It Is: A creamy or firm cornmeal dish, often served as a side to stews or grilled meats.
How It's Served: Commonly paired with venison ragout, mushrooms, or cheese.

Venison Stew:

What It Is: Slow-cooked venison with herbs, red wine, and juniper berries.

Why It's Special: Reflects the Dolomites' hunting traditions and robust flavors.

Spätzle:What It Is: Small, soft egg noodles, often green from spinach.

Best Pairing: Served with cream sauces or melted cheese.

Gröstl:

What It Is: A hearty skillet dish of potatoes, onions, and speck, topped with a fried egg.

Perfect For: A filling lunch after a morning hike or ski session.

Desserts

Apple Strudel:

What It Is: A pastry filled with spiced apples, raisins, and nuts, often served warm.

The Local Twist: Made with South Tyrolean apples and paired with vanilla sauce or cream.

Kaiserschmarrn:

What It Is: Sweet, shredded pancakes dusted with powdered sugar and served with jam or compote.

A Must-Try: Popular in mountain rifugi as a shared dessert or snack.

Strauben:

What It Is: A funnel cake-like treat, fried and dusted with powdered sugar, often served with jam.

When to Try It: Found at markets and festivals.

Zelten:

What It Is: A dense fruitcake made with dried fruits, nuts, and spices.

Seasonal Treat: Traditionally enjoyed during Christmas.

Side Dishes and Snacks

Tirtlen:
What It Is: Fried pastry pockets filled with spinach, ricotta, or sauerkraut.
Perfect For: A quick snack or side dish at Ladin festivals.
Mountain Cheeses:
What It Is: Locally produced cheeses like Stelvio DOP, Graukäse, and Pustertaler.
How to Enjoy: On a cheese platter with honey and walnuts.

Drinks to Pair With Your Meal

Local Wines: Pair your meal with Lagrein (red) or Gewürztraminer (white).
Beers: Try a Forst lager or a craft beer from a local brewery.
Digestifs: End with a glass of grappa or herbal schnapps.

Local Wines and Beers

The Dolomites, located in the South Tyrol and Trentino regions of Italy, boast a rich tradition of winemaking and brewing. With a unique blend of Italian and Alpine influences, the area produces exceptional wines and beers that reflect the region's diverse culture and terroir. Whether you're a wine connoisseur or a casual beer enthusiast, there's something to savor in this mountain paradise.

Local Wines

Lagrein (Red):
Profile: A bold, full-bodied red wine with flavors of dark fruit, spice, and a touch of earthiness.
Pairs Well With: Game meats, pasta with hearty sauces, and aged cheeses.

Where to Try It: Vineyards near Bolzano and Caldaro are renowned for this variety.

Gewürztraminer (White):
Profile: An aromatic white wine with notes of lychee, rose petals, and exotic spices.
Pairs Well With: Asian dishes, white meats, or as a refreshing aperitif.
Fun Fact: Gewürztraminer originated in the village of Tramin in South Tyrol.

Schiava (Red):
Profile: A light, fruity red wine with soft tannins and flavors of cherry and raspberry.
Pairs Well With: Speck (cured ham), charcuterie boards, and simple pasta dishes.
Where to Try It: Widely produced in the Alto Adige region.

Müller-Thurgau (White):
Profile: A crisp, aromatic white wine with citrus and floral notes.
Pairs Well With: Fresh mountain trout, vegetable dishes, and alpine cheeses.
Where to Try It: Popular in higher-altitude vineyards in Trentino and South Tyrol.

Teroldego Rotaliano (Red):
Profile: A robust red wine with dark berry flavors, hints of licorice, and good acidity.
Pairs Well With: Grilled meats, polenta, and mushroom dishes.
Where to Try It: Produced primarily in the Trentino region.

Local Beers

Forst Brewery:
Overview: One of South Tyrol's oldest and most famous breweries, Forst produces a range of beers from light lagers to full-bodied bocks.
Must-Try: Forst Kronen (a classic lager) and Forst Sixtus (a rich double bock).
Where to Enjoy: Visit the Forst Brewery in Lagundo, near Merano, for tastings.

Batzen Bräu:
Overview: A craft brewery in Bolzano offering innovative takes on traditional beer styles.
Must-Try: Their IPA and Weissbier (wheat beer) are particularly popular.
Where to Enjoy: The Batzen Bräu tavern in Bolzano pairs their beers with delicious local dishes.

Pustertaler Freiheit:
Overview: A small brewery in the Puster Valley focusing on unfiltered, organic beers.
Must-Try: Their Pilsner and Kellerbier are favorites for their refreshing taste and crisp finish.
Where to Enjoy: Available at select local bars and restaurants.

Hubenbauer Brewery:
Overview: A family-run brewery and inn in Varna, combining traditional brewing with modern techniques.
Must-Try: Their Dunkel (dark beer) and seasonal specialties.
Extras: You can stay overnight and pair their beers with farm-to-table dishes.

Flea Beer:
Overview: A newer craft brewery gaining popularity for its creative brewing methods and bold flavors.

Must-Try: Seasonal ales and experimental brews like honey beer.

Where to Experience Local Wines and Beers

Wine Roads:
South Tyrolean Wine Road: Explore vineyards and wineries from Bolzano to Caldaro. Many offer guided tastings and vineyard tours.
Trentino Wine Route: Focused on Teroldego and Müller-Thurgau, this route highlights the region's unique wines and scenic landscapes.

Taverns and Bars:
Traditional alpine huts (rifugi) and local taverns often serve both regional wines and craft beers alongside hearty mountain dishes.

Festivals and Events:
Merano WineFestival: A premier event showcasing local and international wines.
Forst Beer Garden (Lagundo): A festive spot to sample Forst brews in a lively setting.

Tips for Trying Local Drinks
Ask for Pairings: Local restaurants and rifugi often recommend wines or beers that perfectly complement their dishes.

Visit a Winery or Brewery: Many producers offer tours where you can learn about their craft and sample their products.

Bring Some Home: Purchase a bottle of Lagrein or a few Forst beers as a souvenir of your Dolomites adventure.

The Dolomites' local wines and beers offer a perfect reflection of the region's unique culture and landscapes. Whether sipping a glass of Gewürztraminer or enjoying a pint of Forst after a day on the slopes, you're sure to taste the spirit of this remarkable area.

Best Restaurants in the Region

The Dolomites offer a rich culinary experience, blending Italian, Tyrolean, and Ladin influences. From Michelin-starred fine dining to cozy alpine rifugi, the region's restaurants serve exceptional dishes with a focus on local ingredients and traditional flavors.

Michelin-Starred Restaurants

St. Hubertus (San Cassiano, Alta Badia)
Why It's Special: A three-Michelin-starred restaurant led by Chef Norbert Niederkofler, renowned for his "Cook the Mountain" philosophy, which emphasizes sustainable, local ingredients.
Must-Try: Tasting menus featuring inventive dishes like venison tartare and foraged herbs.
Atmosphere: Elegant and intimate, perfect for a special occasion.

Restaurant Terra (Sarentino, South Tyrol)
Why It's Special: A two-Michelin-starred gem nestled in a remote mountain setting.
Must-Try: Seasonal tasting menus showcasing creative use of regional ingredients.
Atmosphere: Rustic yet refined, with spectacular views.

La Stüa de Michil (Corvara, Alta Badia)
Why It's Special: A one-Michelin-starred restaurant known for its cozy, wood-paneled dining room and impeccable service.
Must-Try: Gourmet takes on traditional dishes, such as Ladin-style ravioli.
Atmosphere: Warm and welcoming, with a blend of luxury and tradition.

Aquila Nera (Ortisei, Val Gardena)
Why It's Special: Combines contemporary techniques with classic Ladin flavors, earning a Michelin star for its innovative approach.
Must-Try: Locally sourced lamb dishes and creative desserts.
Atmosphere: Sleek and modern, with a focus on culinary artistry.

Traditional Alpine Restaurants

Rifugio Fienile Monte (Alpe di Siusi)
Why It's Special: A cozy mountain hut serving authentic South Tyrolean dishes.
Must-Try: Polenta with venison ragout and homemade strudel.
Atmosphere: Rustic and casual, with stunning views of the surrounding peaks.

Gostner Schwaige (Alpe di Siusi)
Why It's Special: Known for its creative use of flowers and herbs in traditional dishes.
Must-Try: Hay soup and homemade cheese dumplings.
Atmosphere: Quaint and family-friendly, with outdoor seating.

Rifugio Lagazuoi (Passo Falzarego)
Why It's Special: A high-altitude rifugio with panoramic views and hearty food.

Must-Try: Speck, goulash soup, and freshly baked apple strudel.

Atmosphere: Simple and welcoming, with a focus on the surrounding natural beauty.

Modern and Casual Dining

Adlerkeller (Ortisei, Val Gardena)

Why It's Special: A modern twist on traditional Tyrolean cuisine.

Must-Try: Cheese fondue and venison carpaccio.

Atmosphere: Stylish yet relaxed, ideal for families or casual dinners.

Restaurant Tilia (Dobbiaco)

Why It's Special: Combines local ingredients with global culinary techniques.

Must-Try: Trout tartare and locally sourced beef dishes.

Atmosphere: Minimalist and refined, with a focus on flavor and presentation.

Pizzeria Tiroler Stube (Cortina d'Ampezzo)

Why It's Special: A family-friendly spot offering traditional pizza and pasta dishes.

Must-Try: Wood-fired pizza and homemade lasagna.

Atmosphere: Cozy and casual, with warm service.

Wine and Fine Dining Combos

Enoteca Valentini (Ortisei, Val Gardena)

Why It's Special: A wine lover's paradise with a menu designed to pair perfectly with South Tyrolean wines.

Must-Try: Tasting plates featuring local cheeses, cured meats, and seasonal produce.

Atmosphere: Intimate and inviting, ideal for a relaxed evening.

Ristorante Ciasa Salares (San Cassiano, Alta Badia)
Why It's Special: A gourmet restaurant with an exceptional wine cellar and cheese room.
Must-Try: Multi-course tasting menus showcasing local flavors.
Atmosphere: Luxurious yet unpretentious, with a focus on hospitality.

Hidden Gems

Maso Runch (San Cassiano)
Why It's Special: A family-run farm-to-table restaurant offering traditional Ladin meals.
Must-Try: Canederli (dumplings), barley soup, and spätzle.
Atmosphere: Rustic and authentic, with a cozy farmhouse feel.

Baita Sofie (Seceda)
Why It's Special: A charming mountain hut accessible by hiking or skiing.
Must-Try: Kaiserschmarrn (sweet shredded pancakes) and speck.
Atmosphere: Warm and inviting, with breathtaking mountain views.

Ristorante El Brite de Larieto (Cortina d'Ampezzo):
Why It's Special: Focuses on sustainability and local ingredients sourced from its farm.
Must-Try: Homemade cheeses and lamb dishes.
Atmosphere: Rustic yet elegant, with a strong connection to nature.

Tips for Dining in the Dolomites

Reservations: Many popular restaurants, especially Michelin-starred ones, require advance bookings.

Local Specialties: Don't miss regional dishes like speck, polenta, canederli, and apple strudel.

Wine Pairings: Ask for local wine recommendations, particularly Lagrein or Gewürztraminer.

Seasonal Menus: Many restaurants change their menus seasonally to reflect fresh, local ingredients.

Whether you're indulging in fine dining or enjoying a rustic meal in a mountain hut, the Dolomites offer a culinary journey that perfectly complements their stunning natural beauty.

Tips for Foodies Exploring the Dolomites

The Dolomites are a paradise for food lovers, offering a unique blend of Italian, Tyrolean, and Ladin culinary traditions. Whether you're seeking Michelin-starred dining or rustic alpine fare, these tips will help you make the most of your gastronomic adventure.

Explore Local Specialties

Must-Try Dishes:

Speck: Smoked and cured ham, often served with bread or in dumplings.

Canederli: Bread dumplings, typically flavored with speck or cheese.

Polenta: A hearty cornmeal dish served with stews or mushrooms.

Kaiserschmarrn: Sweet shredded pancakes, a favorite dessert.

Cheese to Taste: Try locally produced varieties like Graukäse, Pustertaler, and Stelvio DOP.

Visit Local Markets

Why Go: Regional markets are a treasure trove of fresh produce, artisanal cheese, cured meats, and local wines.

Top Picks:
Bolzano's Market Square (*Piazza delle Erbe*).
Bressanone's weekly market for seasonal specialties.
Brunico Christmas Market (in winter) for festive treats.

Pair Food with Regional Drinks

Wines to Try:
Red: Lagrein, Schiava, and Teroldego Rotaliano.
White: Gewürztraminer and Müller-Thurgau.

Local Beers:
Try brews from Forst Brewery or craft options from Batzen Bräu.
Spirits: Grappa and herbal schnapps (like gentian) are popular post-meal digestives.

Dine at Rifugi (Mountain Huts)
Why It's Special: Rifugi serve hearty, traditional meals in a cozy alpine setting.
What to Order: Polenta with venison ragout, goulash soup, or apple strudel.
Tips: Many rifugi are only accessible by hiking or skiing, making the meal even more rewarding.

Try Michelin-Starred Dining

Top Restaurants:

St. Hubertus (San Cassiano): Known for its sustainable "Cook the Mountain" philosophy.
Terra (Sarentino): Celebrated for its innovative use of local ingredients.
La Stüa de Michil (Corvara): Combines Ladin tradition with fine dining.
Book in Advance: Reservations are essential, especially during high seasons.

Attend Food Festivals

Events to Watch For:
Törggelen (Autumn): Celebrate the harvest season with wine, chestnuts, and hearty Ladin dishes.
Speck Festival (Val di Funes): A celebration of South Tyrol's beloved cured ham.
Merano WineFestival: An international showcase of wines and regional delicacies.

Take a Cooking Class
Why It's Fun: Learn to prepare traditional dishes like dumplings or fresh pasta.

Where to Go:
Ladin farmhouses in Alta Badia often host workshops.
Check with hotels like Rosa Alpina, which offer culinary experiences.

Discover Farm-to-Table Dining
What to Expect: Meals crafted from fresh, local ingredients, often sourced from the restaurant's own farm.
Recommended Spots:
El Brite de Larieto (Cortina d'Ampezzo): Known for sustainable and seasonal menus.

Maso Runch (San Cassiano): A rustisetting with authentic Ladin dishes.

Local Desserts to Try:
Apple strudel made with South Tyrol's famous apples.
Strauben: Fried dough served with powdered sugar and jam.
Zelten: A traditional fruit and nut cake,popular during Christmas.

Plan for Seasonal Menus

Why It Matters: Many restaurants and rifugi change their menus seasonally, showcasing the best ingredients of the time.
What's Seasonal:
Spring: Wild herbs, asparagus, and fresh cheeses.Summer: Berries, mushrooms, and alpine flowers.
Autumn: Chestnuts, pumpkins, and game meats.
Winter: Hearty stews, root vegetables, and festive baked goods.

Seek Out Hidden Gems

Tips for Finding Them:

Ask locals for recommendations.Venture into smaller villages for authentic, family-run trattorias and taverns.

Hidden Gem Examples:

Baita Sofie (Seceda): A scenic mountain hut with traditional dishes.
Gostner Schwaige (Alpe di Siusi): Famous for its hay soup and creative use of flowers.

Savor the Experience

Take Your Time: Meals in the Dolomites are about more than food—they're a chance to relax, enjoy the view, and connect with the culture.

Share a Platter: Many traditional meals are designed for sharing, so don't hesitate to try a little of everything.

Foodies will find the Dolomites a culinary treasure trove, with unforgettable flavors, stunning settings, and a deep connection to the region's culture and traditions.

WHERE TO STAY

Cozy Chalets and Luxury Hotels in the Dolomites

The Dolomites offer a range of accommodations to suit every traveler, from cozy, rustic chalets to luxurious hotels with world-class amenities. Whether you're seeking a tranquil mountain retreat or an indulgent stay with spa services and gourmet dining, here are some of the best options

Cozy Chalets

Chalet Fogajard (Madonna di Campiglio):
Why Stay Here: A secluded eco-friendly chalet surrounded by nature, offering stunning views of the Brenta Dolomites.
Features: Rustic wood interiors, a cozy fireplace, and homemade meals.

Perfect For: Couples or families looking for a peaceful getaway.

Dolomiti Chalet Family Hotel (Trento):
Why Stay Here: Ideal for families, with spacious rooms and child-friendly amenities.
Features: Kids' play areas, guided family hikes, and hearty local meals.
Perfect For: Families with children who want outdoor activities and relaxation.

Chalet al Lago (Lago di Misurina):

Why Stay Here: Located on the shores of Lake Misurina, this chalet offers tranquil lakeside views.
Features: Comfortable rooms, a panoramic terrace, and nearby hiking trails.
Perfect For: Travelers looking for a serene lakeside retreat.

Chalet Planvart (Alta Badia):
Why Stay Here: A traditional Ladin-style chalet with modern comforts.
Features: Self-catering apartments, private balconies, and ski-in/ski-out access.
Perfect For: Small groups or families who value privacy and flexibility.

Mountain Chalet Pia (Val Gardena):
Why Stay Here: Located near hiking trails and ski slopes, with cozy interiors and breathtaking views.
Features: Fully equipped kitchens, sauna access, and a welcoming alpine ambiance.
Perfect For: Adventurous travelers who want a mix of comfort and outdoor fun.

Luxury Hotels

Rosa Alpina Hotel & Spa (San Cassiano, Alta Badia):

Why Stay Here: A 5-star hotel blending luxury with mountain charm, famous for its Michelin-starred restaurant, St. Hubertus.

Features: Elegant rooms, a wellness center, and private excursions.

Perfect For: Gourmet travelers and those seeking a premium experience.

Alpina Dolomites Lodge (Alpe di Siusi):

Why Stay Here: A modern eco-luxury lodge with panoramic views of Seiser Alm.

Features: Spacious suites, a spa with indoor and outdoor pools, and direct access to hiking and ski trails.

Perfect For: Couples or families looking for high-end relaxation.

Cristallo, a Luxury Collection Resort & Spa (Cortina d'Ampezzo):

Why Stay Here: A historic luxury hotel offering elegance and world-class amenities.

Features: Gourmet dining, a full-service spa, and stunning views of the Dolomites.

Perfect For: Those seeking an iconic luxury experience in a vibrant mountain town.

Hotel Ciasa Salares (San Cassiano, Alta Badia):

Why Stay Here: Known for its excellent wine cellar and cheese room, along with luxurious rooms and impeccable service.

Features: Fine dining, wellness facilities, and a cozy yet refined atmosphere.

Perfect For: Food lovers and spa enthusiasts.

Forestis (Bressanone):
Why Stay Here: A minimalist luxury retreat nestled in the Plose mountains, perfect for those seeking tranquility and nature.
Features: Floor-to-ceiling windows, private terraces, and a holistic wellness program.
Perfect For: Couples and solo travelers looking to unwind in style.

Tips for Choosing Accommodations

Location Matters:
For skiing, stay in resorts like Val Gardena, Alta Badia, or Cortina d'Ampezzo.
For hiking, consider Alpe di Siusi or Val di Funes.

Book Early: Luxury hotels and popular chalets fill up quickly, especially during peak seasons (winter and summer).

Consider Amenities: Look for properties with spas, on-site dining, or family-friendly features if those are important to your stay.

B&Bs and Budget-Friendly Options in the Dolomites

The Dolomites offer plenty of charming and affordable accommodations, from cozy bed-and-breakfasts to budget-friendly hotels and guesthouses. These options provide comfortable stays without compromising on warm hospitality or stunning mountain views.

Charming Bed & Breakfasts

Garni La Vara (Corvara, Alta Badia):
Why Stay Here: A family-run B&B with a cozy atmosphere, located near ski lifts and hiking trails.
Features: Comfortable rooms, homemade breakfasts, and friendly hosts.
Perfect For: Skiers and hikers seeking affordability and convenience.

Villa Luise (Ortisei, Val Gardena):
Why Stay Here: Offers simple, clean rooms with breathtaking views of the Dolomites.

Features: Homemade breakfasts, a garden, and proximity to the Seceda cable car.

Perfect For: Couples or solo travelers exploring Val Gardena.

Garni Erna Mountain B&B (San Vigilio di Marebbe):
Why Stay Here: A welcoming B&B with modern amenities and a peaceful setting.

Features: A wellness area, hearty breakfasts, and easy access to the Kronplatz ski area.

Perfect For: Those looking for an affordable yet relaxing stay.

Garni Villa Maria (Selva di Val Gardena):
Why Stay Here: A charming B&B located close to the Sellaronda ski circuit.

Features: Simple, cozy rooms and a delicious breakfast spread.
Perfect For: Ski enthusiasts and families.

Chalet Garni Piz d'Ora (Canazei, Val di Fassa):

Why Stay Here: A traditional B&B with panoramic mountain views and warm hospitality.
Features: Comfortable rooms and a convenient location near hiking trails and ski slopes.
Perfect For: Budget-conscious travelers who want a classic alpine experience

Budget-Friendly Hotels and Guesthouses

Hotel Dolomiti Madonna (Ortisei, Val Gardena):
Why Stay Here: A centrally located hotel offering affordable rates with comfortable amenities.
Features: Simple rooms, on-site dining, and a short walk to lifts and trails.
Perfect For: Travelers seeking value in a prime location.

Hotel Stella Alpina (Moena, Val di Fassa):
Why Stay Here: A budget-friendly option in the charming village of Moena, close to ski and hiking areas.
Features: Friendly service, clean rooms, and a hearty breakfast.
Perfect For: Families and couples exploring Val di Fassa.

Pension Panorama (Dobbiaco, Val Pusteria):
Why Stay Here: An affordable guesthouse with stunning views and a relaxed atmosphere.
Features: Free parking, bike rentals, and a delicious breakfast buffet.
Perfect For: Nature lovers and those seeking tranquility.

Albergo Garni Barancio (Misurina):
Why Stay Here: A simple and affordable hotel near the famous Lago di Misurina.
Features: Cozy rooms, mountain views, and proximity to outdoor activities.

Perfect For: Travelers exploring the Tre Cime di Lavaredo area on a budget.

Garni Schenk (Selva di Val Gardena):
Why Stay Here: A budget-friendly hotel near the ski slopes and hiking trails.
Features: Comfortable rooms, a hearty breakfast, and easy access to the Sellaronda.
Perfect For: Active travelers looking for convenience at an affordable price.

Farm Stays (Agriturismo)

For a unique and budget-friendly experience, consider staying at a traditional farm. These accommodations often include homemade meals and a chance to experience rural life.

Agriturismo Maso Runch (San Cassiano):
Offers authentic Ladin cuisine and comfortable rooms in a rustic setting.

Agriturismo Gasserhof (Bressanone):
A family-friendly farm with opportunities to interact with animals and enjoy homemade products.

Hostels and Budget Apartments

Ostello della Gioventù (Cortina d'Ampezzo):
A clean and affordable hostel with dormitories and private rooms, ideal for solo travelers.

Apartment Rentals:
Websites like Airbnb and Booking.com offer budget-friendly apartments in villages like Ortisei, Canazei, and Corvara.

These are great options for families or groups who prefer self-catering.

Tips for Budget-Friendly StaysBook Early: Budget accommodations fill up quickly during peak seasons (winter and summer).

Look for Deals: Many hotels and B&Bs offer discounts for longer stays or off-season bookings.

Consider Meal Options: Staying at a place that offers breakfast or has a kitchen can help save on dining costs.

Stay in Smaller Villages: Accommodations outside major hubs like Cortina or Ortisei tend to be more affordable

Unique Stays: Rifugios and Farmhouses in the Dolomites

For an unforgettable experience in the Dolomites, consider staying in a *rifugio* (mountain hut) or a traditional farmhouse. These unique accommodations offer a closer connection to nature, authentic local charm, and an escape from the ordinary.

Rifugios (Mountain Huts)

Rifugios provide a cozy retreat for hikers, skiers, and adventurers exploring the Dolomites. Many are perched high in the mountains, offering breathtaking views and hearty meals.

Top Rifugios to Stay In

Rifugio Lagazuoi (Passo Falzarego):

Why Stay Here: Famous for its panoramic views and the largest wood-fired sauna in the Dolomites.

Features: Dormitory-style and private rooms, traditional meals, and sunrise vistas.

Perfect For: Hikers exploring World War I history and nearby trails.

Rifugio Auronzo (Tre Cime di Lavaredo):

Why Stay Here: Located near the iconic Tre Cime peaks, with easy access to popular trails.

Features: Comfortable rooms, a restaurant, and incredible star-gazing opportunities.

Perfect For: Families and beginners looking to experience mountain magic.

Rifugio Puez (Puez-Odle Nature Park):

Why Stay Here: A remote hut surrounded by pristine alpine scenery.

Features: Rustic accommodations, simple meals, and an ideal base for trekking.

Perfect For: Adventurers seeking solitude and serenity.

Rifugio Firenze (Val Gardena):

Why Stay Here: Combines a cozy alpine atmosphere with stunning views of the Odle peaks.

Features: Dorms and private rooms, family-friendly dining, and proximity to easy hiking trails.

Perfect For: Families and nature lovers.

Rifugio Nuvolau (Passo Giau):

Why Stay Here: One of the oldest rifugi in the Dolomites, offering dramatic views from its lofty perch.**Features:** Dormitory accommodations, basic facilities, and rustic charm.

Perfect For: Sunrise enthusiasts and photographers.

Farmhouses (Agriturismi)

Staying at a farmhouse offers a unique opportunity to experience rural life in the Dolomites. Many *agriturismi* serve fresh, homemade meals with ingredients sourced from their own farms.

Top Farmhouses to Stay In

Maso Runch (San Cassiano, Alta Badia):
Why Stay Here: A traditional Ladin farmhouse offering cozy accommodations and authentic meals.
Features: Rustic charm, family-style dining, and activities like farm tours.
Perfect For: Families and food lovers.

Agriturismo Gasserhof (Bressanone):
Why Stay Here: A family-friendly farmhouse with breathtaking valley views.
Features: Spacious rooms, access to hiking trails, and farm-fresh breakfasts.
Perfect For: Nature enthusiasts and those traveling with kids.

Agriturismo Lüch de Survisc (Val Gardena):
Why Stay Here: A working farm with charming accommodations in the heart of the Dolomites.
Features: Fresh dairy products, hands-on farm experiences, and proximity to skiing and hiking.

Perfect For: Families or couples seeking a tranquil retreat.
Hof Unterschweig (Val Sarentino):
Why Stay Here: A secluded farmhouse offering peace and authentic Tyrolean hospitality.

Features: Homemade cheese, fresh eggs, and guided nature walks.
Perfect For: Couples or solo travelers looking to recharge in nature.

Oberfelsonnerhof (Val Pusteria):
Why Stay Here: Nestled in the Puster Valley, this farmhouse offers panoramic views and a warm atmosphere.
Features: Homegrown produce, cozy rooms, and proximity to cycling routes.
Perfect For: Budget-conscious travelers who love rural charm.

Why Stay in a Rifugio or Farmhouse?

Authentic Atmosphere: Experience the traditions and hospitality of the Dolomites.
Proximity to Nature: Enjoy direct access to hiking, skiing, and breathtaking landscapes.
Delicious Local Food: Many rifugi and farmhouses serve fresh, locally sourced meals.
Memorable Views: Waking up to sunrise over the peaks or a peaceful valley is unforgettable.

Tips for Booking Unique Stays

Book Early: Rifugi and agriturismi fill up quickly, especially in peak seasons.
Pack Smart: Rifugi often have shared bathrooms and no Wi-Fi, so bring essentials like toiletries and a headlamp.
Ask About Meals: Many accommodations include meals; confirm dietary options if needed.
Stay Flexible: Rifugi often require hikes or cable car rides to access, so plan accordingly not only a good night's sleep but

also an unforgettable connection to the mountains and their tradition.

CULTURAL EXPERIENCES

Ladin Culture and Traditions in the Dolomites

The Ladin people are an indigenous community of the Dolomites, with a rich cultural heritage that has been preserved for centuries. Spread across regions like Val Gardena, Alta Badia, Val di Fassa, Livinallongo, and Ampezzo, Ladin culture reflects a unique blend of Tyrolean, Italian, and Alpine influences.

Who Are the Ladins?

Origins: The Ladins are descendants of the ancient Rhaeto-Romanic people, who inhabited the region during the Roman Empire.

Language: Ladin is a Romance language still spoken in many Dolomite valleys. While it has some similarities to Italian and French, it is a distinct language with various dialects.

Identity: Despite being a minority group, the Ladins take great pride in their language, traditions, and connection to the mountains.

Ladin Traditions\

Woodcarving:

Significance: Woodcarving is a centuries-old craft in Ladin culture, particularly in Val Gardena. Initially tied to religious art, it has evolved to include sculptures, toys, and decorative pieces.

Experience: Visit workshops in Ortisei or Selva di Val Gardena to see artisans at work

.

Tip: Purchase a handmade figurine or nativity set as a unique keepsake.

Traditional Dress:
Occasions: Ladin clothing is worn during festivals, weddings, and cultural events.

Features: Women wear intricately embroidered blouses, colorful skirts, and velvet bodices, while men don leather breeches and felt hats adorned with feathers.

Cuisine:
Signature Dishes: Ladin cuisine is hearty and simple, featuring ingredients like barley, potatoes, and dairy.
Canederli (dumplings)
Turtres (fried pastries filled with spinach or sauerkraut)
Furtaies (sweet fried spirals)

Experience: Enjoy Ladin specialties at *masi* (farmhouses) or during cultural festivals.

Music and Dance:
Tradition: Folk music and dance are central to Ladin celebrations, often accompanied by accordion and string instruments.
Tip: Look for performances during events like the St. Anne Festival in Alta Badia or Christmas markets.0

Top Cultural Experiences

Ladin Museum (San Martino in Badia):
What It Offers: A comprehensive look at Ladin history, language, and daily life, including exhibits on traditional farming and crafts.
Don't Miss: The section on Ladin legends and mythology.

Viles (Traditional Villages):
What They Are: Small Ladin hamlets with clustered wooden houses and stone barns.
Where to Visit: Explore villages like Longiarù or Colfosco for a glimpse into traditional Ladin life.

St. Anne Festival (Alta Badia):
When It Happens: Held annually in late July.
Why Go: A lively celebration featuring traditional dress, music, and Ladin food.

Sotciastel Archaeological Site (Val Badia):
What It Is: Ruins of an ancient Ladin settlement dating back to the Bronze Age.
Why It's Special: A fascinating window into the early history of the Ladin people.

Christmas Markets:
Where: Bolzano, Ortisei, and San Candido.
What to Expect: Handcrafted Ladin ornaments, woodcarvings, and traditional holiday treats like *zelten* (fruitcake).

Ladin Legends and Folklore
Ladin culture is rich with mythical stories, often tied to the Dolomites' dramatic landscapes.

The Pale Mountains: A famous legend tells how the Dolomites gained their light color, involving a moon prince, a sun princess, and magical dwarves weaving moonlight.

Witches of Sciliar: Stories of witches gathering on the Sciliar Massif during storms are part of local folklore.

Learning Ladin Language
Common Phrases:
Bun dé! (Good day!)
Grazia! (Thank you!)
Ci vedëi! (See you!)

Where to Learn: Cultural centers and guided tours often introduce basic Ladin phrases.

Tips for Experiencing Ladin Culture

Join Guided Tours: Many Ladin villages offer cultural tours led by locals who share stories and insights.

Attend Festivals: Festivals are the best way to experience traditional dress, music, and food in a lively setting.
Support Local Artisans: Purchase handmade crafts and goods from Ladin communities to support their heritage.

Festivals and Events Throughout the Year

The Dolomites come alive with festivals and events that celebrate their unique blend of Ladin, Italian, and Tyrolean traditions. From harvest festivals and skiing events to Christmas markets and summer concerts, there's always something to enjoy, no matter the season.

Winter Festivals and Events

Christmas Markets (Late November–December):
Where: Bolzano, Bressanone, Brunico, Cortina d'Ampezzo.

What to Expect: Festive stalls selling handmade ornaments, local crafts, mulled wine, and traditional treats like *zelten* (fruitcake).

Why Go: The markets are magical, set against the snowy Dolomites with twinkling lights and carolers.

FIS Alpine Ski World Cup (December):
Where: Val Gardena and Alta Badia.

What to Expect: Thrilling downhill and giant slalom races featuring top skiers from around the world.

Why Go: Experience the excitement of world-class skiing with an electric atmosphere.

San Nicolò Parade (December 5th):Where: Val Gardena and surrounding Ladin villages.

What to Expect: A parade led by St. Nicholas and his companion, Krampus, with gifts for children and plenty of festive cheer.

Why Go: A unique Ladin twist on the classic Christmas tradition.

Spring Festivals and Events

Easter Markets (March–April):
Where: Bolzano, Merano.

What to Expect: Seasonal crafts, local delicacies, and beautifully decorated Easter eggs.

Why Go: A quieter yet charming alternative to the Christmas markets.

Flower Festivals (May):
Where: Val di Fassa, Val Gardena, and Alpe di Siusi.

What to Expect: Celebrations of the blooming wildflowers, with guided hikes, botanical tours, and local food stalls.

Why Go: Perfect for nature lovers and families.

Summer Festivals and Events

Maratona dles Dolomites (First Sunday in July):
Where: Alta Badia.

What to Expect: One of the most famous cycling races in Europe, with routes through the scenic Dolomite passes.

Why Go: Even if you're not a cyclist, the event has a festive vibe with plenty of spectator spots.

St. Anne Festival (Late July):
Where: San Cassiano and Alta Badia.

What to Expect: A traditional Ladin festival featuring folk music, dancing, and locals in traditional dress.

Why Go: A unique chance to experience Ladin culture up close.

Sounds of the Dolomites (July–August):
Where: Various mountain locations, including Val di Fiemme and Trentino
What to Expect: Outdoor concerts featuring classical, jazz, and folk music performed in breathtaking alpine settings.
Why Go: Combine a hike with live music for an unforgettable experience.

Speck Festival (September):
Where: Val di Funes.

What to Expect: A celebration of South Tyrol's famous smoked ham with tastings, cooking demonstrations, and live entertainment.

Why Go: Food lovers won't want to miss this deliciously unique event.

Autumn Festivals and Events

Törggelen (October–November):
Where: Throughout South Tyrol, especially around Bolzano and Merano.

What to Expect: A harvest tradition featuring wine tastings, roasted chestnuts, and Ladin dishes like dumplings and polenta.

Why Go: A cozy and authentic way to enjoy the season's bounty.

Merano Grape Festival (October):
Where: Merano.
What to Expect: A celebration of the grape harvest with parades, folk music, and wine tastings.

Why Go: Highlights the region's viticulture and festive spirit.

Transhumance Festival (September):
Where: Val di Fassa and Val Gardena.

What to Expect: Watch as livestock return from high pastures, celebrated with music, food, and local crafts.

Why Go: A colorful event showcasing rural traditions.

Year-Round Highlights
Ladin Carnivals (February or March):
Where: Val Gardena, Val di Fassa, and Alta Badia.

What to Expect: Colorful parades, masked dances, and traditional Ladin folk performances.

Why Go: Experience the Dolomites' playful and cultural side during carnival season.

Farmers' Markets (Weekly):
Where: Towns like Bolzano, Brunico, and Cortina.

What to Expect: Fresh produce, artisanal cheeses, speck, and handmade crafts.

Why Go: A great way to sample local flavors and shop for unique souvenirs.

Culinary Events:
Alta Badia "A Taste for Skiing" (Winter): Michelin-starred chefs create dishes served at mountain huts.

Val Gardena Gourmet Festival (Summer): Celebrates local cuisine with tastings and cooking demonstrations.

Tips for Enjoying Festivals in the Dolomites

Plan Ahead: Many events, especially popular ones like the Maratona dles Dolomites or Christmas markets, require early reservations for accommodations.

Dress Appropriately: Check the weather and wear comfortable clothing, especially for outdoor events.

Learn Local Customs: Embrace Ladin traditions by trying local dishes, greeting people in Ladin (*Bun dé!*), and joining dances.
Combine Activities: Pair a festival visit with hiking, cycling, or sightseeing to maximize your experience.

Museums and Historical Sites

The Dolomites are rich in history, from their geological formation millions of years ago to their cultural and wartime significance. Visiting the region's museums and historical sites offers fascinating insights into its heritage, geology, and traditions

Top Museums

South Tyrol Museum of Archaeology (Bolzano):
Why Visit: Home of Ötzi the Iceman, a 5,300-year-old mummy discovered in the Alps.

Highlights: Exhibits on Ötzi's life, tools, and clothing, alongside artifacts from South Tyrol's prehistoric periods.

Perfect For: History buffs and families with curious kids.

Ladin Museum (San Martino in Badia):
Why Visit: A deep dive into Ladin culture, history, and language.
Highlights: Traditional costumes, tools, and information about Ladin legends and daily life.

Perfect For: Learning about the Dolomites' indigenous community.

Messner Mountain Museums (Various Locations):
Why Visit: A network of six museums created by legendary mountaineer Reinhold Messner, each focusing on a unique aspect of mountain culture.

Key Locations:

MMM Firmian (Bolzano): The central museum about man's relationship with mountains.

MMM Dolomites (Monte Rite): Dedicated to Dolomite geology and mountaineering.

MMM Ortles (Solda): Focuses on glaciers and the icy extremes of mountaineering.
Perfect For: Adventure seekers and mountaineering enthusiasts.

Museum Gherdëina (Ortisei, Val Gardena):
Why Visit: Highlights the natural and cultural history of Val Gardena.

Highlights: Fossils, wooden toys, and traditional Ladin artifacts.

Perfect For: Families and those interested in local crafts.

WWI Open-Air Museums (Lagazuoi and Cinque Torri):
Why Visit: Explore preserved trenches, tunnels, and fortifications from World War I.

Highlights: Guided tours and breathtaking views of the battle-scarred landscapes.

Perfect For: History enthusiasts and outdoor adventurers.

Geological and Natural History Sites
Geoparc Bletterbach (Aldino):
Why Visit: Known as the "Grand Canyon of South Tyrol," this UNESCO World Heritage site showcases millions of years of geological history.

Highlights: Hiking through layers of rock, fossils, and educational exhibits at the visitor center.

Perfect For: Geology lovers and families.

Paleontological Museum (Predazzo):
Why Visit: Focuses on the formation of the Dolomites and its ancient marine origins.
Highlights: Fossilized coral reefs and marine creatures from 250 million years ago.
Perfect For: Science and nature enthusiasts.

Castles and Historical Sites

Runkelstein Castle (Bolzano):

Why Visit: A medieval castle known for its well-preserved frescoes depicting courtly life.

Highlights: Guided tours, a charming courtyard, and stunning views of Bolzano.

Perfect For: Art and history lovers.

Castle Tyrol (Merano):

Why Visit: The ancestral seat of the Counts of Tyrol, offering a glimpse into medieval life.

Highlights: Exhibits on Tyrolean history and breathtaking views of the surrounding valley.
Perfect For: Families and medieval history fans.

WWI Memorial at Passo Pordoi:
Why Visit: A somber reminder of the soldiers who fought in the Dolomites during World War I.

Highlights: Monument and ossuary surrounded by stunning mountain scenery.

Perfect For: Reflecting on history in a breathtaking setting.

Unique Cultural Spots

Sotciastel Archaeological Site (Val Badia):
Why Visit: Explore the remains of a Bronze Age Ladin settlement.

Highlights: Guided tours of ancient walls and artifacts that provide insight into early alpine life.

Perfect For: Those curious about pre-Roman history.

Church of St. Magdalena (Val di Funes):
Why Visit: An iconic church set against the dramatic backdrop of the Odle Peaks.

Highlights: Its picturesque exterior and serene interior make it a popular photo spot.

Perfect For: Photographers and cultural explorers.

Abbey of Novacella (Bressanone):
Why Visit: A historic monastery with a rich history and beautiful baroque architecture.

Highlights: A library, wine cellar, and guided tours of its ornate interiors.

Perfect For: Architecture and wine enthusiasts.

Tips for Visiting Museums and Historical Sites

Check Opening Times: Many museums and sites have seasonal hours, especially in winter.

Book Ahead: Guided tours at popular spots like Messner Mountain Museums or WWI sites may require reservations.

Combine Activities: Pair visits with nearby hikes or scenic drives to make the most of your day.

Ask for Family Discounts: Many sites offer reduced admission for children or family passes.

Exploring the museums and historical sites in the Dolomites offers a deeper understanding of the region's natural wonders, cultural heritage, and historical significance. Whether you're fascinated by ancient artifacts or wartime stories, there's a wealth of discoveries waiting in these mountains.

PRACTICAL TIPS

Understanding Local Etiquette in the Dolomites

The Dolomites are a culturally diverse region influenced by Italian, Germanic, and Ladin traditions. Understanding local etiquette can help you navigate social situations with ease and ensure a warm reception from the friendly locals.

Key Cultural Norms

Greetings and Politeness:

Formal Greetings: A handshake or a slight nod is appropriate when meeting someone for the first time. Use formal titles like *Signore* (Mr.), *Signora* (Mrs.), or *Signorina* (Miss) until invited to use first names.

Common Phrases:
Bun dé! (Good day! in Ladin)
Buongiorno! (Good morning in Italian)
Guten Tag! (Good day in German)
Goodbyes: A friendly *arrivederci* (Italian) or *auf Wiedersehen* (German) is appreciated when parting.

Respect for Tradition:
Dress Appropriately: When visiting churches or religious sites, ensure your shoulders and knees are covered.

Cultural Festivals: Show interest and respect during local festivals by observing or participating politely.

Dining Etiquette:
Timing: Meals are leisurely; don't rush. Lunch (12:30–2:30 PM) and dinner (7:30–9:30 PM) are common dining times.

Tipping: Tipping is appreciated but not mandatory. Rounding up the bill or leaving 5–10% for exceptional service is customary.

Punctuality: If invited to a meal or event, arriving on time is appreciated.

Language Sensitivity:
Multilingual Region: People in the Dolomites may speak Italian, German, and Ladin. Learning a few phrases in each language shows respect and can be a conversation starter.

Don't Assume Language Preference: When addressing someone, use a neutral greeting like *Hello!* or ask, *Parla italiano o tedesco?* (Do you speak Italian or German?).

Outdoor and Environmental Etiquette

Respect Nature:
Leave No Trace: Take your trash with you and avoid picking flowers or disturbing wildlife.

Stay on Trails: Stick to marked paths to protect the delicate alpine ecosystem.

Mountain Rifugios:
Booking in Advance: Rifugios are popular; reserve your spot ahead of time, especially during peak season.

Shared Spaces: Be mindful of noise and personal space in dormitories.**Meals:** Many rifugios serve communal meals; enjoy the opportunity to meet fellow travelers.

Skiing and Hiking Etiquette:

On the Slopes: Follow the International Ski Federation (FIS) rules, including yielding to downhill skiers.

On Trails: Greet fellow hikers with a nod or a friendly *Bun dé!* and step aside to let faster hikers pass.

Cultural Faux Pas to AvoidLoud Behavior:
Keep your voice low in public spaces like restaurants, public transport, or small villagesto respect the serene atmosphere.

Assuming One Culture Dominates:
The Dolomites' blend of Italian, Germanic, and Ladin cultures is a source of pride. Avoid generalizations or favoring one over the others.

Rushing Meals or Service:

Dining is an experience here. Avoid asking for the bill immediately after eating; it's customary to relax and enjoy the moment.

Tips for Making a Great Impression
Show Interest in Local Culture:
Ask questions about Ladin traditions or the region's history. Locals appreciate genuine curiosity.

Dress Neatly:
Casual but tidy clothing is suitable for most situations. Avoid overly revealing attire unless at a beach or spa.

Support Local Businesses:
Purchase handcrafted goods or dine at family-run establishments to show appreciation for the local economy.

Summary of Do's and Don'ts

Do:

Use polite greetings and learn basic phrases in Italian, German, or Ladin.

Respect local traditions and nature.

Participate in cultural events with interest and humility.

Don't:

Assume everyone speaks your language.

Disrespect the quiet, serene atmosphere of villages and trails.

Rush through meals or overlook the region's multilingual identity.

Weather and Safety Considerations in the Dolomites

The Dolomites are known for their stunning landscapes, but the region's alpine environment can present unique challenges. Understanding the weather patterns and taking precautions can help ensure a safe and enjoyable trip.

Weather Patterns in the Dolomites

Seasonal Weather:
Winter (December–February): Cold temperatures, frequent snowfall, and excellent conditions for skiing and snowboarding.
Temperature: -10°C to 5°C (14°F to 41°F).

Spring (March–May): Unpredictable weather with a mix of lingering snow, rain, and blossoming wildflowers.
Temperature: 0°C to 15°C (32°F to 59°F).

Summer (June–August): Warm days and cool nights, ideal for hiking and outdoor activities. Afternoon thunderstorms are common.
Temperature: 10°C to 25°C (50°F to 77°F).
Autumn (September–November): Cooler temperatures, colorful foliage, and quieter trails. Early snow is possible.
Temperature: 5°C to 15°C (41°F to 59°F).

Rapid Changes:
Weather in the mountains can change quickly. Always be prepared for sudden drops in temperature or unexpected storms, even in summer.

Altitude Effects:
Higher altitudes are colder and windier than valleys. Temperatures can drop significantly as you ascend.

Safety Considerations

Hiking and Outdoor Safety:
Plan Ahead: Research trail conditions, difficulty levels, and weather forecasts before heading out.
Dress Appropriately: Wear layers, including waterproof and windproof outerwear. Sturdy hiking boots are essential.

Carry Essentials: Bring a map, compass or GPS, water, snacks, a first-aid kit, and a fully charged phone or power bank.

Start Early: Begin hikes in the morning to avoid afternoon storms, especially in summer.

Know Your Limits: Choose trails that match your fitness level and experience.

Winter Sports Safety:

Stay on Marked Runs: Stick to groomed slopes and respect ski area boundaries.

Wear a Helmet: Always wear a helmet while skiing or snowboarding.

Avalanche Awareness: Check avalanche risks if skiing or snowshoeing off-piste. Carry a beacon, probe, and shovel if venturing into backcountry areas.

Learn Basic Safety: Familiarize yourself with the International Ski Federation (FIS) rules.

Altitude Sickness:
Symptoms: Headache, nausea, dizziness, and shortness of breath.
Prevention: Ascend gradually, stay hydrated, and avoid alcohol. Descend if symptoms persist.

Weather Hazards:
Thunderstorms: Common in summer afternoons. Avoid exposed ridges and peaks during storms; seek shelter if you hear thunder.

Snow and Ice: Can occur in high-altitude areas even in summer. Use appropriate gear like crampons or hiking poles.

Emergency Preparedness

Know Emergency Numbers:
General Emergency Number: 112
Mountain Rescue: 118

Inform Someone of Your Plans:
Share your itinerary with your hotel or a travel companion, especially if venturing into remote areas.

First Aid Knowledge:
Learn basic first aid and carry a kit with essentials like bandages, antiseptic, and pain relievers.

Use Apps for Safety:

Download apps like Komoot or Maps.me for offline trail navigation. Consider apps like "112 Where ARE U" for quick emergency location sharing.

Packing Essentials for Safety

Year-Round Essentials:
Layered clothing, waterproof jacket, sturdy boots.
Sunscreen, sunglasses, and a hat.
Snacks and plenty of water.

Winter-Specific Gear:
Insulated layers, gloves, and a thermal hat.
Avalanche safety gear for off-piste activities.

Summer-Specific Gear:
Lightweight, breathable clothing.
Rain gear and a quick-dry towel.

Travel Insurance

Ensure your insurance covers outdoor activities like skiing, hiking, and climbing.

Check if it includes helicopter rescue, which can be costly in mountain regions.

Money-Saving Tips for Travelers in the Dolomites

Traveling in the Dolomites can be affordable with some smart planning. From finding budget-friendly accommodations to saving on activities and meals, these tips will help you enjoy this stunning region without overspending.

Travel in the Shoulder Seasons

When to Visit:
Late spring (May–June) and early autumn (September–October) offer lower prices on accommodations and fewer crowds.

Why It Saves Money:

Hotels and rifugios often lower rates, and activities like skiing or hiking are less expensive outside peak seasons.

Stay in Budget-Friendly Accommodations

Options to Consider:
B&Bs and Guesthouses: Cozy, family-run accommodations often include breakfast.

Farm Stays (Agriturismo): Affordable rooms with homemade meals included.

Rifugios (Mountain Huts): Great for hikers, offering basic dormitory stays and meals.

Self-Catering Apartments: Save on meals by cooking your own food.

Pro Tip: Look for accommodations in smaller villages rather than popular hubs like Cortina or Bolzano for better rates.

Use Public Transportation
Trains and Buses:
Regional trains and buses connect major towns and villages at a fraction of the cost of renting a car.

Special Passes:
The **Südtirol Mobilcard** offers unlimited travel on regional trains and buses for 1, 3, or 7 days.

Pro Tip: Plan your hikes and activities around accessible routes to avoid expensive transfers or parking fees.

Save on Food and Drinks
Eat Where Locals Eat:

Look for small, family-run trattorias or pizzerias in villages for affordable and authentic meals.
Rifugi Meals: Mountain huts offer hearty, reasonably priced meals like polenta, dumplings, and pasta.

Supermarkets for Snacks:
Stock up on snacks, water, and picnic supplies from local grocery stores.
Avoid Tourist Markups:
Skip dining at restaurants in high-traffic tourist spots, where prices are often inflated.

5. Save on Activities
Free Outdoor Activities:
Hiking, cycling, and exploring scenic spots like Lago di Braies or Val di Funes are free or low-cost.

Ski Passes:
Check for discounted passes, such as multi-day or group options for the **Dolomiti Superski** area.

Guided Tours:
Compare prices for guided activities or consider self-guided options using maps or apps like Komoot.

Local Events:
Look for free or low-cost festivals, markets, or outdoor concerts happening during your visit.

6. Bring Your Own Gear

Why It Helps:
Renting outdoor gear like skis, snowshoes, or bikes can add up quickly. Bringing your own saves money.

What to Pack:
Hiking boots, waterproof jackets, and any specialty gear you might need for planned activities.

Avoid ATM Fees and Currency Exchange Markups
Use Local ATMs: Avoid currency exchange kiosks, which often charge higher fees.
Withdraw larger amounts at once to minimize transaction fees.

No-Fee Cards:
Use credit cards or debit cards with no foreign transaction fees.

Book in Advance

Accommodations:
Secure the best rates by booking hotels, rifugios, or apartments early, especially for high season.

Activities:
Many guided tours, ski passes, and cable car tickets are cheaper when purchased online ahead of time.

Look for Free or Discounted Cultural Experiences

Museum Passes:
The **Museumobil Card** combines free entry to over 90 museums in South Tyrol with unlimited public transportation.

Churches and Historical Sites:
Many beautiful churches and historical landmarks are free to visit or ask for a small donation.

Travel with a Group

Why It Saves:
Splitting the cost of accommodations, car rentals, and meals can significantly reduce individual expenses.

Pro Tip: Choose apartments or chalets with kitchens to cook group meals.

Cluster Activities:
Organize activities in nearby areas to reduce transport costs. For example, explore Alta Badia for a few days before moving to Val Gardena.

Multi-Day Passes:
For extended stays, consider passes like the Dolomiti Supersummer Card (for cable cars) or Dolomiti Superski Pass.

Use Local Apps and Websites
Find Deals:
Check regional tourism websites or apps for discounts on accommodations, events, and transport.

Weather Updates:
Avoid spending on canceled activities by checking reliable weather forecasts for the mountains.

Essential Italian and Ladin Phrases for Travelers in the Dolomites

The Dolomites are a multilingual region where Italian, German, and Ladin are commonly spoken. Learning a few key phrases in Italian and Ladin not only helps you navigate the area but also shows respect for the local culture. Here are some handy phrases to enhance your trip.

Italian is widely spoken throughout the Dolomites, especially in major towns and tourist areas.

Greetings and Politeness

- Hello: *Ciao* (informal), *Buongiorno* (formal, good morning)
- Good evening: *Buonasera*
- Goodbye: *Arrivederci*
- Please: *Per favore*
- Thank you: *Grazie*
- You're welcome: *Prego*
- Excuse me: *Mi scusi*
- I'm sorry: *Mi dispiace*

Basic Questions

- Do you speak English?: *Parla inglese?*
- How much does it cost?: *Quanto costa?*

- Where is the bathroom?: *Dov'è il bagno?*
- Can you help me?: *Può aiutarmi?*

Dining and Food

- I would like...: *Vorrei...*
- A table for two, please: *Un tavolo per due, per favore.*
- Check, please: *Il conto, per favore.*
- Delicious!: *Delizioso!*
- Cheers!: *Salute!*

Directions and Transport

- Where is...?: *Dov'è...?*
- Train station: *La stazione ferroviaria*
- Bus stop: *La fermata dell'autobus*

- Left/Right: *Sinistra/Destra*

- Straight ahead: *Sempre dritto*

Ladin Phrases

Ladin is a Romance language spoken in specific Dolomite valleys, such as Val Gardena, Alta Badia, and Val di Fassa. While not everyone speaks Ladin, using a few phrases can make a great impression.

Greetings and Politeness

- Good day: *Bun dé!*
- Good evening: *Bun domisdé!*
- Goodbye: *Ci vedëi!*
- Please: *Per plasèr*
- Thank you: *Grazia!*
- You're welcome: *Gnente!*

Basic Questions

- What is your name?: *Coj é tu non?*
- My name is...: *Me non é...*
- How are you?: *Co vala?*
- I'm fine, thank you: *Ia sta ben, grazia.*

- Where is...?: *Ndo é...?*

Dining and Food

- I would like...: *Ia vëi...*
- Wine: *Vin*
- Bread: *Pan*
- Water: *Aiva*
- Cheese: *Zëntar*

Directions and Transport

- Where is the trail?: *Ndo é la via?*
- Mountain hut: *La scjëma*
- Left/Right: *Schers/Sterz*
- Straight ahead: *Dritto*

Helpful Tips for Using These Phrases

Start with a Smile: A friendly greeting like *Bun dé!* or *Buongiorno* goes a long way.

Don't Worry About Perfection: Locals appreciate the effort, even if your pronunciation isn't perfect.

Combine with Gestures: If you're unsure of the words, pointing or miming can help.

Learn Local Words: In Ladin-speaking areas, try using Ladin greetings—it's a wonderful way to connect.

SAMPLE ITINERARIES

A Weekend Getaway in the Dolomites

The Dolomites are perfect for a weekend getaway, offering stunning landscapes, outdoor adventures, and cultural experiences in a short amount of time. Here's a 3-day itinerary packed with highlights while leaving enough room to relax and soak in the beauty of the region.

Day 1: Arrival and Scenic Exploration

Morning: Arrival and Check-In

Arrive at your base town, such as **Cortina d'Ampezzo**, **Ortisei**, or **Val Gardena**.

Check into your accommodation (suggestions: cozy chalet, family-run B&B, or a luxury hotel).

Afternoon: Explore Lago di Braies

Drive or take public transport to **Lago di Braies**, one of the most picturesque alpine lakes.

Walk the easy 3.5 km trail around the lake (about 1–1.5 hours).

Rent a rowboat for a serene experience on the turquoise waters.

Evening: Local Dinner

Head back to your base for dinner at a traditional restaurant.

Recommended dishes: *Canederli* (dumplings), polenta with venison, or apple strudel.

Day 2: Adventure and Iconic Views

Morning: Hike or Cable Car Adventure

Option 1: **Seceda Ridgeline Hike (Val Gardena):**
Take the cable car from Ortisei to Seceda.
Hike along the ridgeline for breathtaking views of the Odle Peaks.
Time: 3–4 hours (moderate difficulty).

Option 2: **Tre Cime di Lavaredo Loop:**
Start from Rifugio Auronzo and hike the loop trail around the iconic Three Peaks.
Time: 3–4 hours (moderate difficulty).

Afternoon: Relax at a Rifugio

Enjoy lunch at a mountain rifugio. Try hearty dishes like barley soup or speck platters.

Soak in the panoramic views from the terrace.

Evening: Sunset at Passo Giau

Drive to **Passo Giau**, a high-altitude mountain pass known for its incredible sunset views.

Take photos and relax as the peaks glow in warm hues.

Day 3: Cultural and Leisurely Exploration
Morning: Discover Ladin Culture

Visit the **Ladin Museum** in San Martino in Badia to learn about the region's unique culture and traditions.

Explore nearby traditional villages, such as Longiarù or Colfosco, known for their wooden houses and peaceful atmosphere.

Afternoon: Relax and Farewell Meal

Stroll through a charming town like Ortisei or Cortina d'Ampezzo.

Visit local shops for souvenirs like woodcarvings or alpine honey.

Enjoy a leisurely farewell meal at a family-run restaurant.

Evening: Departure

Head to your departure point (Venice, Verona, or Innsbruck airports, depending on your travel plans).

Tips for a Weekend Getaway

Travel Light: Pack versatile clothing suitable for mountain weather, including layers and comfortable hiking shoes.

Book Ahead: Secure accommodations and any guided tours or activities in advance, especially during peak seasons.

Optimize Transport: If you don't have a car, use regional buses or shuttles to reach key destinations.

7-Day Family-Friendly Adventure in the Dolomites

A week in the Dolomites is perfect for families, offering a mix of outdoor activities, cultural experiences, and relaxation. This itinerary balances adventure with downtime to ensure that everyone, from kids to adults, enjoys the trip.

Day 1: Arrival and Settling In

Morning:

Arrive in **Ortisei** (Val Gardena) or **San Cassiano** (Alta Badia), both excellent family-friendly bases.

Afternoon:

Check into a family-friendly hotel or apartment (*Garni La Vara* or *Cavallino Bianco Family Spa Grand Hotel*).

Take a leisurely stroll around town, explore local shops, and stock up on snacks for the week.

Evening:

Enjoy a casual dinner at a local pizzeria (*Pizzeria L'Murin* in Alta Badia or *Adlerkeller* in Ortisei).

Day 2: Alpe di Siusi – Gentle Adventures

Morning:

Take the cable car from Ortisei or Castelrotto to **Alpe di Siusi**, Europe's largest alpine meadow.

Walk the stroller-friendly trails with breathtaking views of the Sassolungo and Sciliar peaks.

Afternoon:

Have lunch at a rifugio, such as **Gostner Schwaige**, and try the famous hay soup.

Visit nearby playgrounds or relax in the meadows while kids explore.

Evening:

Return to your base and enjoy a relaxing evening.

Day 3: Family Hike and Adventure Park

Morning:

Head to **Val di Funes** and hike the **Adolf Munkel Trail**, a family-friendly path with stunning views of the Odle peaks. (8 km, 3–4 hours).

Afternoon:

Stop by the **Col de Flam Adventure Park** in Val Gardena, which features zip lines, a mini petting zoo, and play areas for kids.

Evening:

Dine at a traditional Ladin restaurant, like **Maso Runch** in Alta Badia, offering kid-friendly meals.

Day 4: Relax and Explore Lago di Braies

Morning:

Drive to **Lago di Braies**, one of the Dolomites' most beautiful lakes.
Walk the 3.5 km flat trail around the lake (stroller-friendly) or rent a rowboat for a fun family activity.

Afternoon:

Have lunch at the lake's restaurant or pack a picnic.
Spend the rest of the day relaxing by the lake or exploring the surrounding area.

Evening:

Return to your base for a quiet evening or enjoy a local gelateria.

Day 5: Cultural Exploration and Easy Trails

Morning:

Visit the **Ladin Museum** in San Martino in Badia to learn about Ladin culture, including traditional clothing and customs.
Stop by a local farm to see animals and sample fresh dairy products (e.g., **Agriturismo Gasserhof**).

Afternoon:

Explore **St. Magdalena Church** in Val di Funes, a picturesque spot with stunning mountain views.
Take a short nature walk in the area to enjoy the serene setting.

Evening:

Return to your accommodation and enjoy a cozy family dinner.

Day 6: Alta Badia – Moviment Parks and Fun

Morning:

Visit the **Moviment Parks** in Alta Badia, accessible via cable cars from La Villa or Corvara.
These mountaintop playgrounds feature slides, climbing structures, and interactive games.

Afternoon:

Have lunch at a mountain rifugio like **Baita Pralongià**, known for its kid-friendly menu and panoramic views.
Spend the afternoon relaxing or enjoying the park's trails and activities.

Evening:

Explore Corvara's charming streets and grab dinner at a family-friendly restaurant.

Day 7: Final Adventure and Departure

Morning:

Take a short hike or scenic drive to **Passo Gardena** for one last stunning view of the Dolomites.
Let kids explore the area and enjoy the fresh mountain air.

Afternoon:

Return to your base, pack, and enjoy a final meal before departing.

Evening:

Head to your departure point (Venice, Innsbruck, or Verona), or extend your stay if time allows.

Family-Friendly Tips

Pack Smart: Bring layers, sunscreen, sturdy shoes, and essentials like snacks and water for hikes.

Plan Activities for Kids: Include interactive stops like adventure parks or farms to keep young travelers engaged.

Take It Slow: Factor in downtime and shorter activities to avoid overtiring kids.

Use Public Transport: Take advantage of regional passes like the **Mobilcard** for free or discounted travel on buses and trains.

Book in Advance: Secure accommodations, cable car tickets, and guided tours early, especially in peak seasons.

10-Day Comprehensive Dolomites Experience

A 10-day itinerary gives you the perfect amount of time to explore the Dolomites' stunning landscapes, experience local culture, and enjoy a mix of adventure and relaxation. This comprehensive guide covers iconic highlights and hidden gems for a balanced, unforgettable trip.

Day 1: Arrival and Bolzano

Morning:

Arrive in Bolzano, the gateway to the Dolomites.
Check into a hotel like **Parkhotel Laurin** or **Hotel Greif**.

Afternoon:

Visit the **South Tyrol Museum of Archaeology** to see Ötzi the Iceman.
Stroll through Bolzano's charming old town and Piazza Walther.

Evening:

Enjoy a traditional Tyrolean meal at **Gasthaus Batzenhäusl**, featuring *speck* and dumplings.

Day 2: Alpe di Siusi

Morning:

Drive or take a cable car to **Alpe di Siusi**, Europe's largest alpine meadow.

Walk the easy trails with views of the Sciliar Massif and Sassolungo.

Afternoon:

Have lunch at a rifugio like **Gostner Schwaige**, known for its hay soup.
Spend the afternoon relaxing or visiting local villages like Castelrotto.

Evening:

Stay overnight in Castelrotto or Ortisei.

Day 3: Val Gardena and Seceda Ridgeline

Morning:

Take the cable car from Ortisei to the **Seceda Ridgeline** for breathtaking views of the Odle Peaks.
Enjoy a moderate hike along the ridgeline (3–4 hours).

Afternoon:

Visit the charming village of **Santa Cristina** and explore local shops.
Optional: Stop by the **Col de Flam Adventure Park** for family-friendly fun.

Evening:

Stay overnight in Val Gardena.

Day 4: Lago di Braies and Val di Funes

Morning:

Drive to **Lago di Braies**, one of the most photographed spots in the Dolomites.
Walk the flat, family-friendly loop around the lake or rent a rowboat.

Afternoon:

Continue to **Val di Funes** and hike the **Adolf Munkel Trail**, offering incredible views of the Odle Peaks.
Visit the iconic **St. Magdalena Church** for picturesque photos.

Evening:

Stay in a cozy farmhouse in Val di Funes or return to Val Gardena.

Day 5: Alta Badia and Ladin Culture

Morning:

Drive to **Alta Badia**, a region rich in Ladin culture.
Visit the **Ladin Museum** in San Martino in Badia to learn about the region's traditions.

Afternoon:

Explore traditional Ladin villages like La Villa or Corvara.

Have lunch at a local restaurant like **Maso Runch**, serving Ladin specialties like *turtres*.

Evening:

Stay overnight in Corvara or San Cassiano.

Day 6: Tre Cime di Lavaredo

Morning:

Drive to **Rifugio Auronzo** and hike the **Tre Cime di Lavaredo Loop** (10 km, 3–4 hours).
Take in iconic views of the Three Peaks and surrounding landscapes.

Afternoon:

Stop by **Lago di Misurina** for a relaxing lakeside stroll.

Evening:

Stay in Cortina d'Ampezzo, known as the "Queen of the Dolomites."

Day 7: Cortina d'Ampezzo and Passo Giau

Morning:

Explore Cortina's charming town center and its boutiques.
Take the cable car to **Tofana di Mezzo** for panoramic mountain views.

Afternoon:

Drive to **Passo Giau**, a stunning mountain pass ideal for photography and short hikes.

Evening:

Stay overnight in Cortina or a nearby rifugio.

Day 8: Marmolada and WWI History

Morning:

Visit **Marmolada**, the highest peak in the Dolomites.
Take the cable car to Punta Rocca for sweeping views of the glacier.

Afternoon:

Explore the **Museum of the Great War**, which highlights the Dolomites' role in WWI.

Evening:

Stay overnight in Arabba or a nearby village.

Day 9: Val di Fassa and Pordoi Pass

Morning:

Drive to **Pordoi Pass** and take the cable car to **Sass Pordoi**, known as the "Terrace of the Dolomites."

Optional: Hike to Rifugio Forcella Pordoi for incredible views.

Afternoon:

Visit **Canazei** or **Moena** in Val di Fassa, exploring their charming streets and local delicacies.

Evening:

Stay overnight in Val di Fassa.

Day 10: Relaxation and Departure

Morning:

Take a leisurely walk or short hike to reflect on your trip.

Suggested areas: Lago di Carezza or a gentle trail in Alpe di Siusi.

Afternoon:

Enjoy a final meal in Bolzano or your departure city.
Depart for home via Venice, Verona, or Innsbruck.

Tips for a 10-Day Trip

Pack Smart: Bring layers, sturdy hiking boots, and weather-appropriate clothing.

Book Early: Reserve accommodations, cable car tickets, and guided tours in advance.

Use Regional Passes: Save on transport with passes like the **Mobilcard** or **Dolomiti Superski Pass**.

Balance Activities: Alternate active hiking days with cultural or leisurely days to avoid exhaustion.

Useful Contacts and Emergency Numbers for the Dolomites

Having important contacts and emergency numbers handy can make your trip to the Dolomites safer and less stressful. Here's a list of essential resources to keep with you during your adventure.

Emergency Numbers

European Emergency Number:
112
This all-purpose number connects you to police, medical, and fire services.

Mountain Rescue:
118
Specifically for emergencies in alpine and remote areas, including hiking or skiing accidents.

Forest Fires Hotline:
1515
Call to report forest fires or environmental hazards.

Medical Assistance

Hospitals and Clinics:
Bolzano Hospital (Ospedale di Bolzano):
Address: Via L. Böhler 5, 39100 Bolzano.
Phone: +39 0471 908111.

Cortina d'Ampezzo Medical Center:
Address: Via Marconi 1, 32043 Cortina d'Ampezzo.
Phone: +39 0436 883361.

Bressanone Hospital (Ospedale di Bressanone):
Address: Via Dante 51, 39042 Bressanone.
Phone: +39 0472 812111.

Pharmacies (Farmacia):
Pharmacies are well-marked with a green cross and often display hours of operation.
Doctor on Call (Guardia Medica):
Phone: 116117 (non-emergency medical assistance).

Tourism Offices

For travel advice, maps, and local information.

Bolzano Tourist Office:

Address: Piazza Walther 8, 39100 Bolzano.
Phone: +39 0471 307000.
Website: bolzano-bozen.it

Val Gardena Tourism Office:
Address: Str. Nives 17, 39048 Selva di Val Gardena.
Phone: +39 0471 777777.
Website: valgardena.it

Cortina d'Ampezzo Tourist Office:
Address: Corso Italia 81, 32043 Cortina d'Ampezzo.
Phone: +39 0436 3231.
Website: cortina.dolomiti.org

Alta Badia Tourism Office:
Address: Str. Col Alt 36, 39033 Corvara.
Phone: +39 0471 836176.
Website: altabadia.org

Trenitalia (Train Services):
Phone: +39 06 3000 (customer service).
Website: trenitalia.com.

Südtirol Mobil (Public Transport in South Tyrol):
Phone: +39 0471 450111.
Website: suedtirolmobil.info.

Dolomiti Bus (Regional Buses):
Phone: +39 0437 941179.
Website: dolomitibus.it.
Taxi Services:
Cortina Taxi: +39 0436 866762.
Alta Badia Taxi: +39 347 317 3513.

Weather and Trail Updates

Dolomites Weather Forecast:
Website: meteo.provincia.bz.it.
Offers up-to-date weather reports and warnings.**Trail Conditions:**
Local tourism offices often provide the latest updates on trail closures or conditions.

Additional Useful Contacts

Carabinieri (Local Police):
Phone: **112**.

Lost Property:
Contact local police stations or the train/bus service where the item was lost.

Helpline for Foreigners in Italy:
Phone: +39 06 4686.
Offers assistance in English and other languages.

Tips for Staying Prepared

Save Numbers in Your Phone: Have key contacts saved and accessible offline.

Carry Insurance Details: Bring travel and health insurance information, including emergency numbers for your insurer.

Download Offline Maps: Use apps like Google Maps or Komoot with offline functionality.
Pack Essentials: Always carry a small first aid kit, water, snacks, and warm clothing for outdoor activities.

Made in the USA
Columbia, SC
06 July 2025

60407870R00093